6-18 81

KNOWLEDGE AND BELIEF

An Introduction to the Logic of the Two Notions

Knowledge and Belief

AN INTRODUCTION TO THE
LOGIC OF THE TWO NOTIONS

By Jaakko Hintikka

UNIVERSITY OF HELSINKI

Cornell University Press

ITHACA AND LONDON

This work has been brought to publication with the
assistance of a grant from the Ford Foundation.

First published 1962 by Cornell University Press.
Published in the United Kingdom by Cornell University Press Ltd.,
2-4 Brook Street, London W1Y 1AA.

Second printing 1964
Third printing 1967
Fourth printing 1969
Fifth printing 1977

Library of Congress Catalog Card Number 62-14461
International Standard Book Number 0-8014-0187-9
Printed in the United States of America

Acknowledgments

THIS work has had the benefit of many kinds of friendly help, intellectual as well as material. Some of its basic ideas date from my tenure of a Junior Fellowship in the Society of Fellows, Harvard University, in 1956–1959. I am glad to have this chance of recording my gratitude to the Society of Fellows for a splendid opportunity to pursue the studies which gave rise to these ideas. The task of developing and articulating them was greatly facilitated by a grant from Valtion Humanistinen Toimikunta, Finland, in 1960. Parts of early versions of this work were read to the Societas Philosophica of Helsinki in September 1959, to the Filosofiska Föreningen of the University of Stockholm in October 1959, and at the graduate and staff seminars of University College, London, in May 1960. My thanks are due to the officers of these institutions for their hospitality, especially to Professor Anders Wedberg and Dr. Stig Kanger in Stockholm as well as to Professor Stuart Hampshire and Mr. Bernard A. O. Williams in London. It is more difficult for me to detail my debts to the

Acknowledgments

individual philosophers with whom I have had the pleasure of discussing some of the subjects of this essay, for their influence on the final version has frequently been indirect. I must mention, in any case, that earlier versions of my work were read and discussed with me by Professors G. H. von Wright and Norman Malcolm, to both of whom I am grateful for many useful suggestions as well as for much pertinent criticism. In Chapter Six the extent of my indebtedness to Professor W. V. O. Quine's lectures and writings should be obvious in spite of my occasional criticism of his views. To a "fellow fellow" at Harvard, Dr. Richard Ohmann, I am indebted for several good examples and for perceptive criticism. Many other friends and acquaintances will find traces of their comments and suggestions incorporated in the text. I hope I may thank them collectively for their contributions and for the inspiration which discussions with them have given me. The responsibility for mistakes of course lies entirely with me. Last but not least I should like to thank Professor Max Black, editor of the series in which this work appears.

JAAKKO HINTIKKA

University of Helsinki
May 1961

Contents

Contents

Three: Model Sets and Model Systems

Four: Problems, Theorems, and Definitions

Contents

Five: Knowing that One Knows

Six: Knowledge, Belief, and Existence

Contents

KNOWLEDGE AND BELIEF

An Introduction to the Logic of the Two Notions

One

Prolegomena

1.1. *Epistemic notions.* The word "logic" which occurs in the subtitle of this work is to be taken seriously. My first aim is to formulate and to defend explicit criteria of consistency for certain sets of statements—criteria which, it is hoped, will be comparable with the criteria of consistency studied in the established branches of logic. What the statements in question are like is also indicated in the title; they are statements made in terms of the following forms of words:

(1) "*a* knows that *p*."
(2) "*a* knows whether *p*."
(3) "*a* does not know that *p*."
(4) "*a* does not know whether *p*."
(5) "*a* believes that *p*."
(6) "It is possible, for all that *a* knows, that *p*."
(7) "It is compatible with everything *a* believes that *p*."

Here *a* is a name of a person or a personal pronoun or perhaps a definite description referring to a human being, and *p* is an independent clause. Double quotes are used in the way Quine uses his quasi quotes ("corners").[1] In other words, by using double quotes we do not refer to the expression which occurs within them. This expression often contains special symbols which refer to names, clauses, or other linguistic entities. The letters '*a*' and '*p*' which occur in (1) are cases in point. When such "syntactical symbols" occur within double quotes, what is referred to is not the expression which the reader sees displayed between the quotes. What is referred to is the result of replacing syntactic symbols by the names, clauses, and so forth, for which they stand. For instance, (1) is the sentence obtained from '*a* knows that *p*' by replacing '*a*' by *a* and '*p*' by *p*. In contradistinction to double quotes, single quotes will be used (as they were just used) to refer purely and simply to the expression which occurs within them. This is in fact the way logicians are accustomed to employ quotes. When there are no syntactic symbols within quotes, the distinction between single and double quotes becomes unimportant. For typographical reasons, we shall in such cases usually prefer double quotes.

The forms of words (1)–(7) will be said to express epistemic notions.[2] In addition to them, the sentences which we shall study may contain propositional connectives like "not," "and," "or," and "only if." The sentences are built by means of these connectives and of (1)–(7) from certain simpler sentences which we do not analyze further in this work and which are called *atomic*

---

[1] W. V. O. Quine, *Mathematical Logic* (rev. ed.; Cambridge, Mass., 1951). See section 6.

[2] The constructions (1)–(7) are of course not the only constructions into which the verbs *know* and *believe* can enter, nor are they the most familiar ones. Some of the other constructions will be analyzed in the course of this work, notably in section 6.3. Others will not be discussed here, although they are likely to have interesting relations to the "basic" epistemic constructions (1)–(7) which constitute the main object of our study.

sentences. Neither quantifiers nor identity are considered until Chapter Six.

It is never too early to try to anticipate and to prevent misunderstanding. The following explanations may therefore be in order: I shall take (6) to mean the same as

"It does not follow from what *a* knows that not-*p*."

In other words, I shall take (6) to be (very nearly) synonymous with

"It is compatible with everything *a* knows that *p*."

From this it is seen that the negation of (6) is not expressed by

"It is impossible, for all that *a* knows, that *p*"

but rather by the sentence

"From what *a* knows it follows that not-*p*"

or, alternatively, by the sentence

"It is incompatible with what *a* knows that *p*."

Notice also that (6) is not synonymous with

"It is possible, to the best of *a*'s knowledge, that *p*."

This sentence speaks of what the case is *to the best of a's knowledge:* in contrast, (6) speaks of what the case is in so far as *a really knows*. There is a difference between the two. Something may be the case to the best of your knowledge and nevertheless turn out not to be so; but you cannot be said really to know what is not the case (cf. section 2.3).

Contrary to the practice of some recent writers, I shall not try to impose any hard and fast distinction between such phrases as

"*a* knows that Cicero denounced Catiline"

and

"Cicero is known by *a* to have denounced Catiline."

1.2. *Statements* v. *sentences.* The initial statement of our aims in 1.1 is in need of explanation and qualification in several respects. First, we have to make up our mind about the distinction between a statement and a sentence. I shall follow what seems to be a fairly established usage, according to which a statement is an event of a certain kind while a sentence is not. More explicitly, a statement is the act of uttering, writing, or otherwise expressing a declarative sentence.[3] A sentence is the form of words which is uttered or written when a statement is made. In order to specify a statement one has to specify the occasion on which it was uttered or written and to specify the speaker or writer. A sentence is specified by specifying the words of which it consists and their order.

The distinction is important because a very good case has been made to the effect that some of the most important logical properties and relations are primarily properties and relations of statements rather than of sentences. It is a statement, and not a sentence, that strictly speaking ought to be said to be true, it

---

[3] A statement is normally addressed to a certain man or certain men· A highly interesting special case arises when the addressee is the same person as the maker of the "statement." Of course this is a very special case; so special, indeed, that you may be reluctant to assimilate it to what we normally call statements. When you address a remark to another man, you have to do something "external"; you have to say or write something or do something else to make your point. In contrast, when you are "addressing yourself," nothing like this is needed. What happens is only the act of trying to persuade yourself of something, i.e., the act of seriously entertaining something in your mind. (Aquinas might have called it an act of thinking something *cum assensu*.) Acts of this kind are not ordinarily called statements. Nevertheless it seems to me that they can be considered as special cases or at least "analogical extensions" of what we do call statements and that some interesting light can be thrown on their logical peculiarities by so doing. For attempts in this direction, see section 4.19 and a paper of mine entitled "*Cogito, Ergo Sum:* Inference or Performance?" *Philosophical Review*, LXXI (1962), 3–32.

has been argued.[4] Accordingly, I shall assume that we are in the first place studying the consistency of certain sets of statements, not the consistency of sets of sentences.

1.3. *Qualifications and limitations.* We cannot hope, however, to study successfully the consistency of arbitrary sets of statements. In order to have some hope of success, the following limitations at least have to be observed:

(a) The statements in question must be made on *one and the same occasion.* The importance of this notion of occasion has not always been properly appreciated. Nevertheless, it is clear that a standard of logical consistency is applicable to a number of statements only when they are fully comparable; and this presupposes, among other things, that the temporal distance between them (including what happens in the interval) is irrelevant. (They must be made within a "logical specious present," as a friend of mine has put it.) I do not know how to characterize this notion of occasion exhaustively. However, the following facts have to be registered: (i) The notion of forgetting is not applicable within the limits of an occasion. (ii) There cannot be any question of increasing one's factual knowledge except, perhaps, by following the logical implications of what one already knows or believes. These restrictions are especially relevant to our present enterprise. For if they are not made, the statements "*a* knows that *p*" and "*a* does not know that *p*" will not be incompatible.

(b) It does not suffice to limit our attention to arbitrary occasions, one at a time, in the ordinary sense of the word. Statements may sometimes be incomparable even though made on one and the same occasion. A case in point is an occasion on which somebody changes his mind. Another is an occasion on which people are engaged in gathering new factual information. Uttered

---

[4] See, e.g., Y. Bar-Hillel, "New Light on the Liar," *Analysis*, XVIII (1957), 1–6.

on such an occasion, the sentences "I don't know whether p" and "I know that p" need not be inconsistent in a natural sense of the word. We must either rule out occasions of these kinds or else stipulate that, in our sense of the term, a new occasion is initiated whenever somebody changes his mind and whenever a new fact is discovered.

(c) If the statements in question contain pronouns in the first person singular, they must be made by one and the same person; if they contain pronouns in the second person singular, they must be addressed to one and the same person; and similarly for the other persons. The rationale of these restrictions is obvious.

(d) To begin with, it is advisable to confine our attention to those properties of classes of statements which depend solely on the sentences they exemplify. Thus we shall in the first few chapters study the consistency of sets of statements only in so far as it turns on the forms of words used. In many ways, this temporary abstention greatly facilitates discussion. Among other things, we may often disregard the distinction between statements and sentences. For instance, we can define the notion of consistency for sets of sentences in addition to sets of statements. Of course, on such a definition the consistency of a set of sentences will only mean that, whenever this set of sentences is uttered (on one and the same occasion by one and the same speaker or writer, addressed to one and the same person, and so forth), then the resulting set of statements is consistent in so far as one can tell without knowing who the speaker is, when the statements were made, or any other facts about them except the forms of words they exemplify.

What this provisional limitation amounts to is easier to see *in casu* than to explain *in abstracto*. Among other things, we are deliberately disregarding the possibility that an inconsistency might be due to the fact that one and the same person is being referred to in more than one way. For instance, we shall not call the sentence "The present British Prime Minister is not a great statesman like Winston Churchill" inconsistent, although the statement made by uttering these words in 1942 or in 1952 could naturally be said to have been self-contradictory. It is worth while to point out that this is not simply due to the presence of the self-referential word "present." The sentence "I know it and I don't know it" is, in our sense, inconsistent, for it *is* inconsistent in so far as one can tell from the form of words alone, in spite of the presence of the self-referential word "I." It may be pointed out, again, that this inconsistency (in our sense) does not mean that this sentence cannot be uttered significantly. It means only that the significance in question has to be gathered from sources other than the literal meaning of the form of words one is using.

There are, however, many logically interesting things to be said about statements which are excluded by the limitation. For instance, there are properties of statements which cannot be defined solely in terms of sentences. In later chapters I shall try to push the analysis a little farther and to define a couple of notions which depend, in addition to the sentences uttered, on certain other things (like the questions who the speaker is and to whom he is addressing his words). This I shall try to do by discussing, among other things, Moore's famous problem of "saying and disbelieving": Why is the sentence

(8) "*p* but I do not believe that *p*"

absurd to utter? I shall also discuss a number of related problems. Among other things, one may compare (8) with

(9) "*p* but I do not know whether *p*"

which sometimes is also somewhat peculiar. I shall suggest an explanation for the strangeness of (8) as well as for the (less marked) peculiarity of (9)—an explanation which also serves to explain why the former is more absurd than the latter.

Knowledge and Belief

1.4. *The plan of this study.* Even after these qualifications, the statement above of our aims is only an approximate one, for the notion of consistency which will be used in our criteria is not self-explanatory. In the sequel we shall supply some further explanations concerning this notion and introduce certain changes in terminology.

After having presented, on the basis of certain general considerations, a number of criteria of consistency, I shall proceed to apply them to a few particular cases. These applications have more than one aim. By their means, I hope to suggest that the results of our general considerations largely agree with the way we naturally use the verbs "to know" and "to believe." I shall also argue that certain apparent exceptions are taken care of by the general qualifications to which our criteria of consistency have to be subjected in any case or that they can otherwise be explained away. Some of the applications seem to have a considerable intrinsic interest. And it was already suggested that some of these applications will lead us to extend our conceptual apparatus in an interesting way.

1.5. *Symbolic notation.* In terms of the notion of consistency, other important notions are easily defined. Following a familiar terminology, I shall call a set of statements *inconsistent* if and only if it is not consistent. I shall call a statement (say p) *valid* if and only if the set $\{``\sim p"\}$ whose only member is the negation "$\sim p$" of p is inconsistent.

For the sake of greater facility of formulation, I shall frequently use (as I have already done to some extent) a concise symbolic notation. In this notation, "K_a" is the formal counterpart of the words "a knows that"; "B_a" the formal counterpart of "a believes that"; "P_a" the counterpart of "it is possible, for all that a knows, that"; and "C_a" the counterpart of "it is compatible with everything *a* knows that." '*K*,' '*B*,' '*P*,' and '*C*' will be called *epistemic operators*. Of the propositional connectives, I shall use '∼,' '&,' 'v,' and '⊃'; *p, q, r, . . . , p₁, q₁, r₁, . . . , p₂, q₂, r₂, . . .* are arbitrary sentences; {*p₁, p₂, p₃, . . .*} is the set which consists of *p₁, p₂, p₃, . . .* ; λ, μ, ν, . . . are arbitrary sets of sentences; and '∊' refers to the relation of membership. It is assumed that '⊃' can always be eliminated in terms of the other connectives in the usual way.

The syntactic expression '∼*p*' (and likewise the expression 'not-*p*' twice employed in section 1.1) naturally does not refer to the mere result of prefixing "not" to *p*. It refers, rather, to the corresponding negative sentence, often referred to as the contradictory of *p*. In the more accurate terms of Chomsky's transformational grammar, '∼*p*' (as well as 'not-*p*') stands for the result of applying the negativizing transformation T_{not} to *p*, which has to be assumed to be given in a suitable form.[5]

1.6. *Formulas v. sentences.* The introduction of our symbolic notation could be reinterpreted as the introduction of the notion of a *formula*. The relation of formulas and the sentences we are studying will then be such that the latter are substitution-instances of the former. (Sentences may be substituted for atomic formulas, names for free individual symbols, and so on.) From this point of view, we can conveniently specify the sentences we are interested in as substitution-instances of the formulas defined (recursively) as follows:

(*i*)   Atomic formulas (whatever they are) are formulas;
(*ii*)   if *p* is a formula, then so is "∼*p*";
(*iii*)   if *p* and *q* are formulas, then so are "(*p* & *q*)" and "*p* v *q*)";

---

[5] Noam Chomsky, *Syntactic Structures* (The Hague, 1957), pp. 61–62, 112.

(iv) if p is a formula and a a free individual symbol, then "$K_a p$," "$P_a p$," "$B_a p$," and "$C_a p$" are formulas. In each case, p is said to be the *scope* of the epistemic operator in question.[6]

We shall assume that the outmost pair of parentheses may be omitted in any formula which is considered independently, that is, not as a part of another formula.

We shall not normally use this interpretation in the sequel, however. Instead of thinking of $p, q, r, \ldots$, as formulas, that is, as placeholders for sentences, we shall usually prefer thinking of them simply as sentences. If the other usage appeals more to the reader, he will find it easy to translate what I shall say into his own jargon. The difference will be largely immaterial in the sequel, and therefore will not always be heeded very strictly.

1.7. *Difficulties of translation.* There arises a preliminary problem of translating (2)–(4) into the symbolic notation. Clearly one knows whether p is true if, and only if, one knows that p is true or knows that p is false. Hence (2) translates as

(2)* "$K_a p \vee K_a \sim p$."

Accordingly, (4) should be translated as

(4)* "$\sim K_a p \ \& \ \sim K_a \sim p$."

Prima facie it is tempting to take (3) to be the mere denial of (1), that is, to translate it as "$\sim K_a p$." However, a moment's reflection shows that in some of the most typical cases (3) is a correct form of words only if p is in fact true. In such cases,

[6] Strictly speaking, we ought to distinguish those free individual symbols which can take only names of persons as their substitution-values and which can therefore serve as subscripts of epistemic operators from those which cannot do so. We do not really need the distinction until Chapter Six, however.

(3) is not the contradictory of (1); it should rather be translated as

(3)* "p & $\sim K_a p$."

The same seems to be the case with the question "Does a know that p ?" This question likewise seems to be correct only when the speaker assumes that p is in fact true.

Neither of these can be taken as a hard and fast rule, however, although they seem to be fairly general rules. Suppose Russell had met a friend sometime in 1918 who had recently had news from Austria. The following exchange would not have been unnatural in the least (as far as logic is concerned): "Is Wittgenstein dead or alive?" "I have heard rumors that he is dead." "Do you know that he is dead?" "No, I don't know that he is dead; the rumors may not be true, for all that I really know." Here the translation (3)* does not work.

When is the translation (3)* of (3) appropriate, and when should we rather translate (3) as "$\sim K_a p$"? One useful point of view is suggested by the history of the expressions we are studying. Originally, we are told, the word "that" in (1) and a fortiori in (3) was a *demonstrative*.[7] Hence (3) was originally construed as "a does not know that: p," that is, as being equivalent to something we should nowadays express as follows:

"p; and a does not know that"

or, in more explicit terms, as follows:

(3)(a)   "It is the case that p; and a does not know that."

It seems to me that we are entitled (history aside) to look for a paraphrase of this kind whenever we encounter a sentence of the

---

[7] See C. T. Onions, *An Advanced English Syntax* (6th ed.; London, 1932), sec. 296. A similar development has taken place in a number of other languages, including German and Finnish.

form (3). Prima facie this requirement seems to bring us back to the requirement that (3) should always be translated as (3)*, and in fact to support it by means of the history of the expressions we are studying. But this is not really the case. It is by no means necessary that the first clause of a paraphrase like (3)(a) should always be in the declarative mood. In different circumstances, the following might be a more natural paraphrase:

(3)(b)   "Is it the case that p? a does not know that."

Where (3)(b) is the best paraphrase of (3), the best translation into our formal notation is not (3)* but rather "$\sim K_a p$." Hence we may, in order to find the right translation of (3) on some particular occasion, try to paraphrase it in the way just indicated and to see in what mood (declarative, interrogative, etc.) the earlier occurrence of p has to be assumed to be to which a demonstrative "that" could refer. To be more precise, we have to ask what would be the mood of the sentence *as uttered by the same speaker* to which a demonstrative "that" could be thought of as referring. For instance, the exchange: "He is a perjurer"—"You don't know that he is; the witnesses you are relying on are untrustworthy" ought to be paraphrased for our purposes as follows: "He is a perjurer"—"Is he? You don't know that; the witnesses. . . ." Here the right translation is clearly of the form "$\sim K_a p$."

Of course, the declarative mood and therefore the translation (3)* is likely to be the most usual one. Normally it is the only possible translation when (3) occurs as a part of ordinary fact-stating discourse. However, our examples show that it need not be the best translation when the question has been raised (explicitly or implicitly) whether p is true.

The possibility of translating (3) into our notation by some expression different from (3)* is particularly important in the case of first-person sentences. For we shall see (in section 4.13) that in this case the translation (3)* is (for reasons we shall discuss later) somewhat unnatural even when the context seems to be that of fact-stating discourse. There is thus a tendency to look for a context of a different kind in this case.

It has to be added that what we have said in this section applies only when the stress pattern of the sentences under discussion is normal (i.e., when there are no emphatic stresses in our sentences). Of the ways in which an emphatic stress may change the logic of our sentences we shall have a brief glimpse later.

The phrase "*a* does not believe that p" has a peculiarity of its own in that it is often used as if it were equivalent to "*a* believes that $\sim p$." In such cases, it is translatable by "$B_a \sim p$" rather than by "$\sim B_a p$."

Two

Criteria of Consistency

2.1. *The actualization of possibilities.* In looking for criteria of consistency, I shall mainly deal with the notion of knowledge; the notion of belief can usually be treated along the same lines.

Let us suppose that someone makes a number of statements on one and the same occasion; and let us suppose that among the sentences he utters there are the following:

"I know that p_1."
"I know that p_2."

. . . . .

"I know that p_k."
"It is possible, for all that I know, that q."

Under what conditions is he consistent? It will be agreed that one condition at least has to be fulfilled, namely, that the following set of sentences is also consistent:

"I know that p_1."
"I know that p_2."

. . . . .

"I know that p_k."

"q is in fact the case."

In other words: If it is consistent of me to say that it is possible, for all that I know, that q is the case, then it must be possible for q to turn out to be the case without invalidating any of my claims to knowledge; that is, there must not be anything inconsistent about a state of affairs in which q is true and in which I know what I say I know.

In formal terms, we may formulate the condition in question as follows:

(A.PKK*) If a set λ of sentences is consistent and if "$K_a p_1$" ϵ λ, "$K_a p_2$" ϵ λ, . . . , "$K_a p_k$" ϵ λ, "$P_a q$" ϵ λ, then the set {"$K_a p_1$," "$K_a p_2$," . . . , "$K_a p_k$," q} is also consistent.

In this work we shall usually assume that this formulation includes the case $k = 0$. This amounts to assuming that whenever something is said to be possible, for all that some particular man knows, then this something is implied to be logically possible *simpliciter*. This assumption may be open to criticism. It certainly seems very implausible when "$P_a q$" is read "It is compatible with everything a knows that q." I am prepared to believe that excluding this case from our formulation of (A.PKK*) might very well be the most natural procedure. Nothing of importance will turn on the acceptance or rejection of this assumption, as far as this work is concerned. Accepting it will merely simplify our subsequent discussion in certain respects.

The rule (A.PKK*) is perhaps the most important rule with which we shall deal in this essay. It is therefore worth while to examine it somewhat more closely.

2.2. *Defending the rule* (A.PKK*). The rule (A.PKK*) may be compared with the weaker rule—we shall call it (A.PK*)—

obtained by replacing the set $\{$"$K_a p_1$," "$K_a p_2$," . . . , "$K_a p_k$," $q\}$ by $\{p_1, p_2, . . . , p_k, q\}$. Why are we justified (as we clearly are) in adopting the stronger rule (A.PKK*) and not only the weaker rule (A.PK*)?

One answer to this question seems to be as follows. That q is the case can be compatible with everything a certain person— let us assume that he is referred to by a—knows only if it cannot be used as an argument to overthrow any true statement of the form "a knows that p." Now this statement can be criticized in two ways. One may either try to show that p is not in fact true or else try to show that the person referred to by a is not in a position or condition to know that it is true. In order to be compatible with everything he knows, q therefore has to be compatible not only with every p which is known to him but also with the truth of all the true statements of the form "a knows that p." And this is exactly what is required by (A.PKK*).

If this explanation is correct, it shows that the applicability of (A.PKK*) is rather allergic to shifts of sense of the verb *know*. It shows that the applicability of (A.PKK*) as distinguished from (A.PK*) presupposes that a statement of the form "a knows that p" can be criticized not only by discussing whether p is true but also by discussing whether the bearer of the term a is in a position or in a condition really to know it. Now the verb *know* is frequently used in such a way that this assumption is not satisfied. In ordinary speech, "knows" often means little more than "is aware" or "rightly believes." [1] Where this is the case,

---

[1] The difference I am inclined to see between the ordinary use of the expression *be aware* and the philosopher's use of the verb *know* may be illustrated as follows: If you have been told that p has happened and if this information is correct, then in the ordinary discourse we should naturally say either that you know that p has happened or that you are aware that it has happened (presupposing of course that you believe what you have been told). It may turn out, however, that the information you had was really insufficient to sustain claim to knowledge

criticism of the second kind loses most of its point. It does not make sense to ask whether somebody is in a position to have a true belief (opinion) on a given topic in the way it makes sense to ask whether he is in a position to know. In such cases (A.PKK *) may become inapplicable, although (A.PK *) of course remains valid. Applications of the former rule may therefore introduce tacit assumptions as to the sense of the occurrence(s) of the verb *know* to which it is applied. We shall have occasion to return to this fact in section 5.8.

It seems to me, nevertheless, that in its most typical sense the verb *know* admits of the rule (A.PKK *). It certainly does so if anything like the analyses philosophers have recently given of the meaning of the verb is correct. (I shall call the sense of *know* they are trying to explicate the "primary" or "full" sense of the word.) If the expression "I know" serves to show that I have all the evidence one could need [2] or if it implies "I have the right to be sure" [3] or if it implies that "I have adequate evidence for the hypothesis (or proposition) in question," [4] then by

---

in the strong sense of the word in which philosophers are wont to use it and in which it is contrasted to true opinion. (It might turn out, e.g., that your source of information, although correct in this particular case, is frequently unreliable.) Then you may have to give up your claim to *knowledge*. Even in such an event, it would nevertheless be very awkward to try to deny that you were *aware of p*'s having happened. Certainly you were not *unaware of* it.

In this footnote I have spoken (for simplicity) of 'knowing that *p*' where it would strictly speaking be more appropriate to speak of 'knowing the truth of *p*' or of 'knowing what *p* expresses.' In the sequel I shall frequently make use of similar locutions.

[2] J. O. Urmson, "Parenthetical Verbs," *Mind*, N.S. LXI (1952), 480–496, reprinted in *Essays in Conceptual Analysis*, ed. by Antony Flew (London, 1956), pp. 192–212. See p. 199.

[3] A. J. Ayer, *The Problem of Knowledge* (Harmondsworth, Middlesex, 1956). See I, *v*.

[4] Roderick M. Chisholm, *Perceiving: A Philosophical Study* (Ithaca, N.Y., 1957). See p. 16.

uttering it I commit myself to defending not only what I say I know but also the fact that I am in a position (in an appropriate "evidential situation," to use a term of Urmson's) to say it. And this means that (A.PKK*) is applicable.

Although I do not want to tie my discussion to any particular philosophical position, I think that the three suggestions just mentioned are also right in stressing that one can be justified in saying "I know" only if one's grounds are "conclusive" or "adequate" in some sense. I am not in a position to say "I know" unless my grounds for saying so are such that they give me the right to disregard any further evidence or information. We must realize, however, that having this right need not mean that one's grounds are so strong that they logically imply that what one claims to know is true.[5] It may merely mean that the grounds one has are such that any further inquiry would be pointless for the normal purposes of the speakers of the language.[6] Whoever says "I know that *p*" proposes to disregard the possibility that further information would lead him to deny that *p* although he could perhaps imagine (logically possible) experiences which could do just that. He is right if he is justified in doing so.

What exactly is implied in the requirement that the grounds of knowledge in the full sense of the word must be *conclusive?* For our purposes it suffices to point out the following obvious consequence of this requirement: If somebody says "I know that *p*" in this strong sense of knowledge, he implicitly denies that any further information would have led him to alter his view. He commits himself to the view that he would still persist in saying that he knows that *p* is true—or at the very least persist

---

[5] Norman Malcolm, "Knowledge and Belief," *Mind*, N.S. LXI (1952), 178–189. See especially pp. 179–180.

[6] Cf. Douglas Arner's able defence of a similar view in his note "On Knowing," *Philosophical Review*, LXVIII (1959), 84–92.

in saying that *p* is in fact true—even if he knew more than he now knows. We shall have occasion to return to this fact in section 3.7.

In any case, this is one possible sense of the verb *know*. It is the sense which my rules are primarily calculated to catch. It seems to me to be primary in the sense that certain other uses of the verb *know* in more or less ordinary discourse can be analyzed by its means.

So far I have discussed the conditions on which one would be right in saying "I know." The discussion also gives us an answer to the question as to when we are right in saying "*a* knows that *p*." We are right if and only if the person referred to by *a* would be right if he said "I know that *p*." This answer need not commit us to the interesting view (which may very well be right) of J. O. Urmson that the uses of the verb *know* in the first person singular (and in the present tense) are logically prior to its other uses. For there can very well obtain such a parallelism between the different uses of "know" even if none of them is logically prior to the others.

This transition from the first person to the third necessitates an interesting qualification to the rule (A.PKK*). We have seen that in this rule it is assumed that the sentence

(1) "*a* knows that *p*"

implies more than that the person referred to by *a* is right in believing that *p* is the case; it is assumed that (1) implies that the person in question is in a position to defend a statement to the effect that he knows that *p* is the case. If *a* is a description or an unfamiliar name, it may happen that the person to whom it in fact refers is nevertheless unwilling to defend a statement of the form (1), although he is able and willing to defend a statement of the form "*I* know that *p*," as made by himself. The reason is not difficult to appreciate: our man may not know that he happens to be referred to by the term *a*. In applying (A.PKK*) we must therefore assume that the person referred to by *a* knows that he is referred to by it, in short, that it is true to say "*a* knows that he is *a*" or, more naturally, "The person who in fact is *a* knows that he is *a*." (Notice that the applications of the rule (A.PK*) are not subject to any qualification of this sort.) The question how this assumption can be formalized will be discussed in Chapter Six. Meanwhile it is important to keep in mind that the assumption is not always satisfied. Even if it were true to say "The greatest fool in Christendom knows that *p*," it would not follow that the person in question would defend a statement of this particular form, although it does follow that he could defend a similar statement in the first person.

2.3. *Further rules.* Most of the other rules I shall set up require less commentary.

(A.K) If λ is consistent and if "$K_a p$" ε λ, then λ + {*p*} is also consistent.

This rule is, I think, perfectly incontestable.[7] However, in order to see its obviousness we must recall what exactly we mean by

---

[7] I am tempted to dub this rule "Parmenides' law." The old man seems to have recognized it when he said that "thou couldst not know that which is not (that is impossible) nor utter it" (Hermann Diels, *Die Fragmente der Vorsokratiker*, 7th ed., fr. 2, lines 7–8, in J. E. Raven's translation). It is interesting to see that it was very natural for Parmenides to go from this (valid) insight to his famous thesis that "that which can be spoken and thought needs must be" fr. 6, line 1; cf. fr. 8, lines 35–36); all he had to do was to replace the verb for knowing (γιγνώσκω) by a verb for thinking (νοέω) and to contraposit. The transition was made particularly seductive by the intertwined meanings of the two Greek verbs. Even the simplest rule of logic, we thus see, may become philosophically interesting when it begins to break down. For another early recognition of the impossibility of "false knowledge," cf. Plato's *Gorgias* 454 D.

consistency. What (A.K) says is merely that whenever you say "*a* knows that *p*" it would be inconsistent *for you* to deny *on that very same occasion* that *p* is the case. What is more, it only says that this is inconsistent provided that you are using words in their literal sense. It does not say anything, for example, of what may be called "inverted-commas" uses of "know," exemplified by such sentences as "All the experts 'knew' Mr. Truman would lose in 1948; but they turned out to be completely wrong."

(A.&)   If λ is consistent and if "*p* & *q*" ε λ, then λ + {*p,q*} is also consistent.

(A.v)   If λ is consistent and if "*p* v *q*" ε λ, then λ + {*p*} or λ + {*q*} is consistent (or both are).

(A.∼)   If *p* ε λ and "∼*p*" ε λ, then λ is inconsistent.

(A.∼&)   If "∼(*p* & *q*)" ε λ and if λ is consistent, then so is the set obtained from λ by replacing "∼(*p* & *q*)" by "(∼*p* v ∼*q*)."

(A.∼v)   If "∼(*p* v *q*)" ε λ and if λ is consistent, then so is the set obtained from λ by replacing "∼(*p* v *q*)" by "(∼*p* & ∼*q*)."

(A.∼∼)   If "∼∼*p*" ε λ and if λ is consistent, then so is the set obtained from λ by replacing "∼∼*p*" by *p*.

It is not difficult to see that the replacements which are mentioned in the last three rules may also be performed when the formulas in question occur as parts of larger formulas, without affecting the consistency or inconsistency of any set of formulas. In the sequel, replacements of this sort are sometimes made tacitly.

The rules whose designation begins with 'A' will be referred to collectively as (A) rules.

2.4.   *Rules for the notion of belief.*   Before we discuss the remaining rules which govern the notion of knowledge we shall in this section briefly discuss the question whether the analogues to the rules we have so far set up are valid for the notion of belief. And before doing that, we shall first note a consequence of the earlier rules for knowledge and make a few notational conventions.

The rules (A.PKK*) and (A.K) together entail the following rule:

> If a set λ of sentences is consistent and if "$K_a p_1$" ϵ λ, "$K_a p_2$" ϵ λ, . . . , "$K_a p_k$" ϵ λ, "$P_a q$" ϵ λ, then the set $\{p_1, p_2, \ldots, p_k,$ "$K_a p_1$," "$K_a p_2$," . . . , "$K_a p_k$," $q\}$ is also consistent.

Here we shall include the case in which q is absent. The analogue to this rule for 'B' and 'C' (replacing 'K' and 'P,' respectively) is called (A.CBB*), while (A.CB*) will be the analogue to (A.PK*) for 'B' and 'C.'

When we are dealing with belief instead of knowledge, the analogue to (A.K) is immediately seen not to be valid. It is also seen at once that (A.CB*) is valid. Since the six rules (A.&) – (A.~~) do not involve the notion of knowledge at all, they naturally remain valid. The difficult question is whether (A.CBB*) is valid.

I shall argue that it is. The arguments which led us to adopt (A.PKK*) seem to me to be applicable, *mutatis mutandis*, also to the notion of belief. If something is compatible with everything you believe, then it must be possible for this something to turn out to be the case together with everything you believe without making it necessary for you to give up any of your beliefs. If your beliefs are to be consistent, it must also be possible for all your beliefs to turn out to be true without forcing you to give up any of them. This corresponds to the case in which q is absent from (A.CBB*). An example may make my point easier to appreciate. Let us consider the following sentences:

"The Laputans believe that they will be attacked by the Ruritanians"

and

"The Laputans believe that the Ruritanians will attack them only if the attack comes as a surprise"

and let us understand the second sentence as meaning the same as

"The Laputans believe that the Ruritanians will attack them only if they do not believe that they will be attacked."

In other words, let us assume that we are given a pair of sentences of the form

(a) "$B_a p$"

and

(b) "$B_a(p \supset \sim B_a p)$"

respectively. It seems to me that the pair of sentences $\{(a), (b)\}$ is clearly inconsistent. The Laputans cannot consistently believe that the only thing they have to be afraid of is a surprise attack. For if this belief were true, their belief that an attack is imminent would imply that they will not be attacked, contrary to what they believe. And the reason for this inconsistency is just what I indicated. The two beliefs (a) and (b) cannot turn out to be true unless the Laputans give up their belief that they will be attacked.

This intuitive inconsistency of the pair $\{(a), (b)\}$ strongly suggests that the rule (A.CBB*) is valid. For it is easy to see that the weaker rule (A.CB*) does not suffice to make the pair of sentences consisting of (a) and (b) inconsistent. (I shall spare you the formal details.) Similar examples are easily constructed to the same effect.

In the sequel, I shall therefore work on the assumption that (A.CBB*) is valid. On certain crucial occasions I shall nevertheless call attention to it when I am using it and indicate whether that particular use might perhaps be dispensed with. We must also remember that the applications of the rule (A.CBB*)— unlike the applications of the rule (A.CB*)—are based on an assumption similar to the assumption which underlies (A.PKK*) (see the end of 2.2): it has to be assumed that the person referred to by *a* believes that he is referred to by it.

A comparison with other "propositional attitudes" shows that the validity of (A.CBB*) really is a nontrivial characteristic of the notion of belief. The analogues to this rule for certain other notions are clearly invalid. A brave but homesick boy might say "I wish I were at home—but I wish that I did not wish it" without being inconsistent. Yet the analogue to this sentence for the notion of belief, namely,

$$``B_a p \ \& \ B_a \sim B_a p"$$

can easily be seen to be inconsistent by means of (A.CBB*), together with (A.&) and (A.$\sim$). <u>Hence the analogue to (A.CBB*) cannot be valid for the notion of wishing.</u>

We must realize, however, that in the same way as some of the senses of *know* in ordinary discourse do not satisfy (A.PKK*) some of the usual senses of *believe* do not satisfy (A.CBB*). Often "*a* believes" says nothing more than "it seems to *a*" or "*a* is under the impression" or "*a* surmises." Then (A.CBB*) is much less plausible than when it expresses conviction or considered opinion. The pair of sentences

(c) "It seems to the Laputans that they will be attacked by the Ruritanians"

and

(d) "It seems to the Laputans that they will be attacked by the Ruritanians only if the attack comes as a surprise" (i.e., only if it does not seem to the Laputans that they will be attacked)

26

is much less objectionable than the pair {(a), (b)}. It is true that all that seems to be the case to the Laputans according to (c) and (d) can turn out really to be the case only if it also turns out that (c) is false. But the Laputans cannot be blamed for inconsistency for this reason. According to (c) it seems to them that they will be attacked, but it does not follow that it seems to them that this is how things seem to them.

Examples of this kind may not strike you as entirely convincing. In the sequel we shall see why it is especially difficult to show that such pairs as {(c), (d)} above and {(e), (f)} below are *not* inconsistent: although they are not inconsistent in the sense we are dealing with here, they may indeed be said to be inconsistent in certain secondary senses of the word. (Cf. section 4.13.)

In spite of this difficulty I shall suggest that examples may also be useful in showing that certain senses of "know" do not follow the rule (A.PKK*), as I argued above on the basis of certain general considerations. For instance, it seems to me that the pair of sentences

(e) "He is paying attention to the fact that the time is running short"

and

(f) "He is not paying attention to the fact that the time is running short while he is paying attention to the fact"

is not as obviously inconsistent as the pair of sentences obtained by replacing "is paying attention to the fact" by "knows." [8] The last-mentioned pair is of the form

$$\{``K_a p,"\ ``\sim K_a(p\ \&\ K_a p)"\}$$

---

[8] In order to avoid trivial inconsistency we must of course understand the "while"-clause of (f) as modifying only the "that"-clause which precedes it. A pair of parentheses would remove the ambiguity: "He is not paying attention to the fact that (the time is running short while he is paying attention to the fact)."

and can be shown to be inconsistent by means of (A.PKK*) but not by means of (A.PK*). In so far as "knows" or "is aware" is used in the same way as "pays attention to the fact," the rule (A.PKK*) is not applicable to them.

That the phrase "is aware" is sometimes used in this way is suggested by the pair of sentences

"He is aware that he is beginning to fall asleep"
and
"He is aware that he is beginning to fall asleep while he is aware of it."

In order for an analogue to the rule (A.PKK*) to be applicable to the phrase "is aware" here we would have to say that the first sentence entails the second. To my mind, it does not.

One way of expressing the gist of the difference between the primary senses of the verbs *know* and *believe* on one hand and those senses of these verbs on the other in which they are tantamount to "pays attention to the fact" or "is aware" and "is under the impression" or "surmises," respectively, is as follows: In the primary sense of *know*, if one knows one *ipso facto* knows that one knows. For exactly the same circumstances would justify one's saying "I know that I know" as would justify one's saying "I know" *simpliciter*. (To this fact, which may seem to violate our intuitions, we shall return in Chapter Five.) In contrast, "I am paying attention to the fact" cannot be made to entail "I am paying attention to the fact that I am paying attention to the fact" as little as "I wish" entails "I wish that I wished." Similarly, "I surmise" or "it seems to me" does not seem to entail "I surmise that I surmise" or "it seems to me that it seems to me," respectively. It also seems to me that "I am aware that" cannot be said to imply "I am aware that I am aware that" in the sense of implication with which we are concerned here. (Cf. section 4.13.)

Criteria of Consistency

Here we can see that one of our examples above was in fact quite unfavorable to our own argument. The example which gave rise to the formulas (a) and (b) was in terms of what a number of people believe. In such a case, it is rather natural to assume that (A.CBB*) fails. The Laputans may believe that they will be attacked by the Ruritanians without therefore believing that they believe it, for each of them may be unaware that the others believe it. Our theory, however, is designed to be applicable to what an individual human being believes (and knows), not to what a number of individuals are said to believe (and know). In the case of an individual a failure of this kind may be taken to be impossible, provided that we have to do with a really considered opinion or belief. Pointing this out may perhaps help the reader to appreciate our reasons for accepting (A.CBB*).

2.5. *Two critical rules.* The remaining rules for the notion of knowledge are critical in the sense that the qualifications to which our analyses have to be subjected are largely due to them:

(A.~K) If λ is consistent and if "$\sim K_a p$" ϵ λ, then $\lambda +$ $\{$"$P_a \sim p$"$\}$ is also consistent.

(A.~P) If λ is consistent and if "$\sim P_a p$" ϵ λ, then $\lambda +$ $\{$"$K_a \sim p$"$\}$ is also consistent.

It is easy to see that instead of (A.~K) and (A.~P) we could equally well have a pair of rules which would authorize us to replace "$\sim K_a p$" by "$P_a \sim p$" and "$\sim P_a p$" by "$K_a \sim p$." Replacements of this kind could also be (and sometimes will be) performed when the formulas in question occur as parts of larger formulas. (Not all such replacements will be explicitly acknowledged.)

It is obvious, from the formal point of view, that some rules like (A.~K) and (A.~P) are indispensable. Since the other rules

29

do not mention sentences of the form "$\sim K_a p$" and "$\sim P_a p$," we have no means of dealing with statements of these forms unless some rules like (A.$\sim$K) and (A.$\sim$P) are adopted.

It is equally obvious, however, that the rules (A.$\sim$K) and (A.$\sim$P) are not unproblematic in the way the previous ones are. We may take the first of the two as an example. It is true, in some sense, that if I utter

(10) "I don't know whether p"

then I am not altogether consistent unless it really is possible, for all that I know, that p fails to be the case. But this notion of consistency is a rather unusual one, for it makes it inconsistent for me to say (10) whenever p is a logical consequence of what I know. Now if this consequence-relation is a distant one, I may fail to know, in a perfectly good sense, that p is the case, for I may fail to see that p follows from what I know. Hence there seems to be a discrepancy between my rules and the way the verb "to know" is actually used.

Another instance of the same apparent discrepancy is constituted by implications of the form

"If he knows that p, then he knows that q"

or, more generally, of the form

(11) "$K_a p \supset K_a q$."

By means of my rules, it is readily seen that (11) is valid as soon as p logically implies q in our ordinary propositional logic. (When my treatment is extended to include quantifiers, the implications studied in the quantification theory will be cases in point as well.) But it is clearly inadmissible to infer "he knows that q" from "he knows that p" solely on the basis of the fact that q follows logically from p, for the person in question may fail to see that p entails q, particularly if p and q are relatively complicated statements. The state of his knowledge might be comparable with that of a man who knows the axioms of some sophisticated mathematical theory but who does not know some distant consequences of the axioms. Nobody would criticize him for inconsistency.

Hence there need not be anything nonsensical, irrational, or dishonest about a set of sentences which I have called inconsistent even when they are uttered by one and the same person on one and the same occasion. They are not inconsistent in any psychological or quasi-psychological sense of the word. They may even be true simultaneously. This does not go to show that our rules are incorrect, however. What it shows is that the notion which they define is unlike inconsistency in the current senses of the word, and should be carefully distinguished from it. It shows, in short, that our terminology is not appropriate.

2.6. *Consistency reinterpreted as defensibility.* What my notion of consistency amounts to in typical cases is *immunity to certain kinds of criticism.* In order to see this, suppose that a man says to you, "I know that p but I don't know whether q" and suppose that p can be shown to entail logically q by means of some argument which he would be willing to accept. Then you can point out to him that what he says he does not know is already implicit in what he claims he knows. If your argument is valid, it is irrational for our man to persist in saying that he does not know whether q is the case. If he is reasonable, you can thus persuade him to retract one of his statements without imparting to him any fresh information beyond certain logical relationships (the rules of which he is assumed to master right from the beginning). You have done this by pointing out to him that he would have come to know that q all by himself if he had followed far enough the consequences of what he already knew.

Immunity to this kind of criticism (or persuasion) seems to me a notion important enough to deserve serious study. We have seen, however, that it is not entirely appropriate to call this notion consistency. I shall therefore adopt or, rather, coin, a few new terms. Instead of consistency and inconsistency, I shall speak of *defensibility* and *indefensibility*, respectively, and instead of valid sentences I shall speak of *self-sustaining* sentences. Whenever an implication "*p* ⊃ *q*" is self-sustaining, I shall say that *p* *virtually implies q*. If *p* virtually implies *q* and vice versa, I shall say that *p* and *q* are *virtually equivalent*.

Of course, the new terms have to be substituted, retroactively, for the old ones in the (A) rules. This change makes it obvious, I hope, that the rules (A.∼K) and (A.∼P) are correct and intuitively acceptable. The former does not say that not knowing that *p* implies "possibly *p*"; it merely says that if I deny knowing that *p*, I am susceptible to the kind of persuasion just described unless it really is possible, for all that I know, that *p* should be the case. And this seems to be perfectly incontestable. In general terms, it may be said that the rules (A.∼K) and (A.∼P) are not concerned with the truth of statements at all; they merely tell us that certain adjunctions always preserve the defensibility of sets of sentences.

Certain warnings are needed here. Our explanation of the meaning of the new terms must not be pressed too hard. In the sense in which we shall use the term, an indefensible sentence is not always one from which its utterer can be dissuaded by the sole means of internal evidence. An indefensible statement can indeed be changed (from true to false) without imparting to anybody any fresh information beyond certain logical relationships, but persuasion of this sort may have to be directed to persons other than the speaker (or writer). The general characteristic of indefensible statements is, therefore, that they depend for their truth on somebody's failure (past, present, or future) to follow the implications of what he knows far enough. (Later, we may have to add, "knows *or* believes.") This, indeed, is in keeping with the spirit of our explanations. If you say "*a* does not know that *p*" when *p* follows from what the person referred to by *a* already knows, you may be right, but you are taking a risk. I can turn your statement from true to false merely by elaborating to your man some of the consequences of the overt information he has; or he can do it by himself.

If the rule (A.PKK*)—as distinguished from (A.PK*)—is to be applicable to what the person referred to by *a* is said to know, we have to assume something more. We have to assume that the persuasion which may be directed against him may be given a somewhat broader basis than was just indicated. We must be able to base the persuasion not only on what he is said to know but on everything he would undertake to defend if he said in so many words, "I know." Among these commitments, it was noted, is the very fact *that* he knows. This assumption is satisfied if by "*a* knows" we mean that he has enough information to say, correctly, "I know." It is not satisfied if "knowing that" merely means being aware of the fact in question.

2.7. *Defensibility and analyticity.* The peculiarities of my basic notions are important enough to deserve some further comments. It may be objected to the explanation just given that it pre-supposes an unwarranted distinction between criticisms which can be based on purely logical grounds and criticisms which can only be made to stick by adducing empirical evidence; in short, it may be objected that I am presupposing the analytic-synthetic distinction which is at best extremely vague.

What is true about these objections is that any notion which is explained as immunity to certain kinds of criticism is no more precise than the standards on which the criticism is based. It may also be true that the general standards of purely logical (analytical) criticism are extraordinarily fluid. Fortunately I do not have to resort to them except in a very limited area. What I need are the standards of criticism applied in the particular contexts (1)–(7). And it is these standards that I have sought to formulate in the (A) rules proposed above. The notion of defensibility is therefore exactly as intuitive or as precise as these rules. Any objections to my notions have to be directed against them. Contrasting the different kinds of criticism only serves to ward off a possible misunderstanding of these rules.

2.8. *The applicability of our results.* The qualifications which I have suggested affect the applicability of our rules and the results that may be obtained by their means. For instance, the fact that a sentence of the form (11) is self-sustaining does not mean that the person referred to by a knows that q as soon as he knows that p. Often it means merely that if he knows that p and pursues the consequences of this item of knowledge far enough he will also come to know that q. Nothing is said about whether anybody will ever do so. In general, our discussion is applicable to what people actually (or, as we shall say, actively) know only to the extent to which they are aware of the consequences of what they know.

It is also seen at once, however, that our results will not be completely unrealistic, that they are to some extent applicable to what people actively know. Or, rather, the virtual implications we are studying are to some extent paralleled by strong pragmatical implications. There are no *logical* reasons why somebody who knows that p should know that q even when q's following from p is perfectly obvious. But such cases are likely to be exceptions. If the consequence is quite obvious, we might even be reluctant to say that he does not know that q, although he denies himself, on being asked, that he knows it; we might be tempted to say instead that he did not understand the question, that he was confused ("caught off guard")—that he "really" knows, or even that he *must* know. Ordinarily, we have every reason to follow up the logical consequences of what we know to some extent, one of them being the fact that, in the eyes of the law, people are presumed to intend (and hence to know) the reasonable and probable consequences of what they knowingly do. But even apart from questions of legal responsibility you do not willingly expose yourself to criticism to which you can only reply by admitting your failure (inability?) to see the implications of what you are saying; unless of course the implications are so remote that one is not normally expected to perceive them.[9] If you say you know that *p* and if *q* obviously follows from *p*, then you are likely to admit that you know that *q*, too. (Notice, incidentally, that this is the case even if you are lying in saying that you know that *p*.) This likelihood is, roughly speaking, the greater the shorter the deductive chain which connects *p* and *q*.

Hence, whenever a virtual implication can be demonstrated by means of a relatively brief argument, we are entitled to expect that it is paralleled by a good pragmatical implication. This is the case even when the speaker cannot himself articulate any step-by-step argument which would prove the implication. For him the implication may be simply a matter of logical or linguistic intuition.[10] Similarly, if a statement can be shown to be inde-

---

[9] The standards of normality presupposed here need not be absolute. When a mathematician writes that something is "easy to see" (witness Laplace's notorious "Il est aisé à voir"), the chances are that his point is not very obvious even for an acute layman to perceive.

[10] It should not be surprising that we can thus "feel" certain logical relationships without being able to articulate them. This is certainly not any more surprising than the fact that we have fairly well-defined intuitions as to what is grammatically correct, although the full explication of the criteria of grammaticalness (say in English) is a large undertaking which has only recently got really started. Cf. Noam Chomsky, *Syntactic Structures* (The Hague, 1957), and a review by R. B. Lees in *Language*, XXXIII (1957), 375–408.

fensible by means of a fairly short piece of reasoning, it is unlikely that anybody should seriously make it. And if this should nevertheless happen, the presumption is that the speaker is using language in some peculiar way explainable in terms of his particular situation rather than in terms pertaining to language at large.

It may also be pointed out that a number of results can be demonstrated without using the critical rules (A.∼K) and (A.∼P). Such results are applicable without the qualifications just mentioned.

The limitations to which our results are usually subject may perhaps also be explained as follows: Our results are not directly applicable to what is true or false in the actual world of ours. They tell us something definite about the truth and falsity of statements only in a world in which everybody follows the consequences of what he knows as far as they lead him. A sentence is self-sustaining if it is true in all such worlds, defensible if it is true in at least one such world, and so on. They are applicable to actual statements only in so far as our world approximates one of the "most knowledgeable of possible worlds," as we may call them, or can be made to approximate one of them by calling people's attention to the consequences of what they know. In fact, from every proof of ours to the effect that a certain sentence is self-sustaining we can read a definite set of directions for making it true by calling the attention of certain people to certain logical connections. If we can show (by means of the rules we have set up or by means of the alternative technique we shall explain in the following chapter) that a sentence can somehow be made true by the sole means of internal criticism, we can also show in detail how this result may be brought about in a finite number of steps.

2.9. *Defensibility and analyticity again.* The qualifications which we have found it necessary to make need not completely dissociate our notions of defensibility, of indefensibility, of self-sustenance, and the like from the current notions of consistency, inconsistency, validity (analyticity), and the like. On the contrary, the observations we have made serve to bring into a sharper focus certain salient facts about the latter group of notions. Whatever necessity there is about logical truths (valid statements) or about relations of logical consequence (entailment) pertains to the subject matter which is being talked about and not to anybody's (active) knowledge thereof. If q is entailed by p, then the state of affairs expressed by p cannot be realized without realizing the state of affairs expressed by q, too. But from this it does not follow, obviously, that anybody who knows that p should for this reason actively know that q, unless it be assumed that he is making the best possible use of his knowledge. Logical truths are not truths which logic forces on us; they are not necessary truths in the sense of being unavoidable. They are not truths we *must* know, but truths which we *can* know without making use of any factual information. The logical implications of what we know do not come to us without any work on our own part; they are truths which we can extract, often with considerable labor, from whatever information we already have. The fact that the so-called laws of logic are not "laws of thought" in the sense of natural laws seems to be generally admitted nowadays. Yet the laws of logic are not laws of thought in the sense of commands, either, except perhaps laws of the sharpest possible thought. Given a number of premises, logic does not tell us what conclusions we ought to draw from them; it merely tells us what conclusions we may draw from them—if we wish and if we are clever enough. When a judge says that people "must" be presumed to know the reasonable consequences of their actions, he does not mean that a particular defendant should have been under the necessity of knowing a certain consequence of what he did. It suffices that the consequence is such that a reasonable man would have known it and that the defendant may have known it. "It is not an inference," a justice has put it (paraphrasing Lord Porter in Lang *v.* Lang [1955] A.C. 402, at p. 427), "that must be drawn, but which may be." This is the case, I submit, with all logical inferences (as such).

The applicability of our results may thus be said to presuppose a certain amount of rationality in the people whose attitudes are being discussed. In this respect, our logical theory is comparable with certain other theories (e.g., the theory of games) which may also be said to depend on an assumption of rationality. The comparison might be worth pursuing further. Be this as it may, the presupposition shows that our results are not applicable to every attitude covered by the word "belief" to an equal extent. Beliefs in the sense of convictions or commitments are much less amenable to rational persuasion than beliefs in the sense of opinions. If it is suggested that we are in this essay really studying the logic of opinion rather than the logic of belief, I shall not object (provided, however, that the qualifications made in section 2.4 are heeded).

2.10. *An alternative interpretation.* There are other ways of interpreting the simple formal system we have set up. So far, we have tried to make sense of it by interpreting in an unconventional way the most important metalogical notions, like those of consistency, validity, and the like. Instead of doing this, we might try to take another course and change the readings of our object-language. It might be suggested that we are not studying the logic of the expressions (1)–(5) directly. Instead, we study the logic of the closely related notions obtained by reading "$K_a p$" as follows:

(12)   "It follows from what *a* knows that *p*." [11]

---

[11] This, of course, is but the sense in which Meno's slave had always known that the square of the diagonal of a square is twice the original

Then "$\sim K_a p$" and "$P_a \sim p$" as well as "$\sim P_a p$" and "$K_a \sim p$" will mean exactly the same, and all our (A) rules are valid without any qualifications. Moreover, it would also be obvious that the results of our discussion are applicable to the expressions (1)–(5) only to the extent to which people actually are aware of the implications of what they actively know.

This approach would probably yield the same results as the first one, if pushed far enough. It leads to certain difficulties, however, which make it less useful than the one we have taken. For instance, reading "$K_a p$" as (12) suggests that we are somehow appealing to some given standard of logical consequence. Far from being true, this suggestion is diametrically opposed to what we are actually doing. For one of the chief tasks of my essay is to formulate, to explain, and to defend certain criteria of logical consistency (my "defensibility") in terms of which criteria of logical consequence (my "virtual" implication) may be defined.

What is more important, in the new approach the applicability of our results to the actual uses people make of the verbs *know* and *believe* would be considerably more problematic than in the first approach. For these reasons, I shall not go any further in this direction.

---

square. Plato was deeply impressed with the possibility of inducing new knowledge in a fellow man without giving him any factual information.

Three

Model Sets and Model Systems

3.1. *Model sets.* In the last few sections of Chapter Two I defended my (A) rules against certain misinterpretations. In this chapter I shall try to defend them by making them more systematic. For this purpose it may be observed that a set λ of sentences can be shown to be indefensible by means of the rules (A.$\sim$), (A.&), (A.v), (A.$\sim\sim$), (A.$\sim$&), and (A.$\sim$v)—with the notion of defensibility replacing that of consistency, of course —if and only if it cannot be imbedded in a set μ of sentences which satisfies the following conditions:[1]

(C.$\sim$)   If $p \ \epsilon \ \mu$, then not "$\sim p$" $\epsilon \ \mu$.

(C.&)   If "p & q" $\epsilon \ \mu$, then $p \ \epsilon \ \mu$ and $q \ \epsilon \ \mu$.

(C.v)   If "p v q" $\epsilon \ \mu$, then $p \ \epsilon \ \mu$ or $q \ \epsilon \ \mu$ (or both).

---

[1] These conditions and those additional conditions which we shall later introduce (and accept) to complement them will be referred to collectively as (C) conditions. The reader's attention is called to the list of frequently mentioned conditions and rules which is given at the end of this work and which he may find useful in checking references and in comparing the different rules and conditions with each other.

(C.∼∼)   If "∼∼p" ε μ, then p ε μ.

(C.∼&)   If "∼(p & q)" ε μ, then "∼p" ε μ or "∼q" ε μ (or both).

(C.∼v)   If "∼(p v q)" ε μ, then "∼p" ε μ and "∼q" ε μ.

This statement will not be given a proof here, as it has been proved elsewhere [2] and as it is fairly plausible without one. I shall point out instead that sets of sentences which satisfy the conditions above have many interesting properties. I have proposed to call them *model sets* (of propositional logic); and I have studied them in some detail elsewhere.[3] For our present purposes, the gist of their formal properties may be expressed in an intuitive form by saying that they constitute, in the absence of logical constants other than propositional connectives, a very good formal counterpart to the informal idea of a (partial) *description of a possible state of affairs.*

In view of this fact it is not surprising that the consistency of a set λ of sentences can be shown to amount to the capacity of λ of being imbedded in a model set. For clearly λ is consistent if and only if there exists a possible state of affairs in which all the members of λ are true, that is, if and only if there is a (consistent) description of a possible state of affairs which includes all the members of λ. Of course, in the form it has been formulated here this result holds only in the absence of logical constants other than the propositional connectives ∼, &, and v. It can be easily generalized, however, beyond propositional logic (e.g., to quantification theory) as we shall see in Chapter Six.

[2] See my article, "A New Approach to Sentential Logic," *Societas Scientiarum Fennica, Commentationes Physico-Mathematicae*, XVII (1953), no. 2.

[3] See my papers, "Form and Content in Quantification Theory," *Acta Philosophica Fennica*, VIII (1955), 7–55, and "Notes of the Quantification Theory," *Societas Scientiarum Fennica, Commentationes Physico-Mathematicae*, XVII (1955), no. 12.

Knowledge and Belief

3.2. *Model systems.* We may develop this heuristic idea further. In doing so, we are led to ask how the properties of model sets are affected by the presence of the notions of knowledge and belief; how, in other words, the notion of model set can be generalized in such a way that the consistency (defensibility) of a set of statements remains tantamount to its capacity of being imbedded in a model set. What additional conditions are needed when the notions of knowledge and belief are present?

Let us suppose that μ is a description of a possible state of affairs; and let us suppose that "$P_a p$" ϵ μ. In more intuitive terms, let us consider a state of affairs in which it is true to say that it is possible, for all that the person referred to by the term a knows, that p. Clearly the content of this statement cannot be adequately expressed by speaking of only one state of affairs. The statement in question can be true only if there is a possible state of affairs in which p would be true: but this state of affairs need not be identical with the one in which the statement was made. A description of such a state of affairs will be called an *alternative to* μ with respect to a. (Sometimes the state of affairs will itself be said to be an alternative to the state of affairs described by μ.)

Hence we have to impose the following condition on a model set μ:

> If "$P_a p$" ϵ μ, then there is at least one alternative μ^* to μ (with respect to a) such that p ϵ μ^*.

This is not quite explicit, however, for it is not obvious what is meant by "there is" here. The situation is as follows: We have seen that, in order to study the properties of sentences which contain the notion of knowledge, it does not suffice to consider a single model set at a time. In order to show that a given set of sentences is defensible, we have to consider a set of model sets.

Model Sets and Systems

Such sets of model sets will be called *model systems*. In terms of this notion we may formulate our condition as follows:

(C.P*)   If "$P_a p$" ϵ μ and if μ belongs to a model system Ω, then there is in Ω at least one alternative μ^* to μ (with respect to a) such that p ϵ μ^*.

The condition (C.P*) serves to make sure that it is possible that p. We required more, however; we required that it is possible, for all that the person referred to by the term a knows, that p. Hence everything he knows in the state of affairs described by μ he also has to know in the alternative state of affairs described by μ^*. In other words, the following condition has to be imposed on the model sets of a given model system:

(C.KK*)   If "$K_a q$" ϵ μ and if μ^* is an alternative to μ (with respect to a) in some model system, then "$K_a q$" ϵ μ^*.

It is obvious that the following condition has to be imposed on model sets:

(C.K)   If "$K_a p$" ϵ μ, then p ϵ μ.

The following pair of conditions can be defended in the same way the corresponding rules (A.$\sim$K) and (A.$\sim$P) were defended in sections 2.6 to 2.10 above:

(C.$\sim$K)   If "$\sim K_a p$" ϵ μ, then "$P_a \sim p$" ϵ μ.
(C.$\sim$P)   If "$\sim P_a p$" ϵ μ, then "$K_a \sim p$" ϵ μ.

3.3.   *The interrelations of our rules and conditions.*   These conditions suffice for our purposes (as long as we do not include new notions, such as quantifiers, within the scope of our discussion). As far as I can see, any further condition which one may be tempted to introduce either turns out to be a consequence of the ones above or else turns out to give rise to absurd (counterintuitive) consequences. Hence we may define the defensibility of a set of sentences as a capacity of being imbedded in a member of a model system. A model system is a set of sets between some of which there obtains a dyadic (two-place) relation, called the relation of alternativeness. Each member of a model system has to satisfy the conditions we formulated in sections 3.1–3.2—with the exception, of course, of the starred conditions (C.P*) and (C.KK*)—and the relation of alternativeness has to be such that (C.P*) and (C.KK*) are satisfied. (No other conditions are needed.) The other notions may be defined in terms of defensibility in the same way as before.

It can be shown that a set of sentences is indefensible in the sense just defined if and only if it can be shown to be indefensible by means of the (A) rules (with "defensible" replacing the term "consistent," of course). It would take us too far, however, to prove this important result here. It will be proved in detail in a planned work of mine on the semantics of modal logic.

Similarly, it may be shown that the force of (C.KK*) over and above that of (C.K*) is exactly the same as the force of (A.PKK*) over and above that of (A.PK*). If it is decided to exclude the case $k = 0$ from the rule (A.PKK*), as we found it possible to do at the end of section 2.2, we must likewise modify the condition (C.P*); we must limit its applicability by requiring that there has to be at least one sentence of the form "$K_a q$" in μ.

3.4. *Alternative conditions.* Instead, we shall here discuss some simple consequences of the conditions which we have set up in this chapter as well as certain alternative ways of formulating them. If the conditions (C.KK*) and (C.K) are satisfied, it is easily seen that the following condition has to be satisfied, too:

(C.K*)   If "$K_a p$" ϵ μ and if μ^* is an alternative to μ (with respect to a) in some model system, then p ϵ μ^*.

Model Sets and Systems

If (C.K*) is used, (C.K) can obviously be replaced by the following condition:

(C.refl)   The relation of alternativeness is reflective.

From (C.refl) it follows that

(C.min)   In every model system each model set has at least one alternative.

From (C.min) and (C.K*) it is seen that the following condition is satisfied:

(C.k*)   If "$K_a p$" ϵ μ and if μ belongs to a model system Ω, then there is in Ω at least one alternative μ^* to μ (with respect to a) such that p ϵ μ^*.

One of these conditions is in terms of the simple logical properties of the relation of alternativeness, namely, (C.refl). It may be asked whether this relation has other properties of this nature. It may be seen that this relation is *not* symmetric. For this purpose, let us recall that a model set μ_2 is an alternative to μ_1 if, and only if, intuitively speaking, there is nothing about the state of affairs described by the former that is incompatible with what someone knows in the state of affairs described by the latter. Now it is obviously not excluded by what I now know that I should know more than I now do. But such additional knowledge may very well be incompatible with what now is still possible, as far as I know.

On the same showing, the relation of alternativeness appears to be transitive. If μ_2 described a state of affairs compatible with all that someone knows in the state of affairs described by μ_1, and if similarly μ_3 describes a state of affairs compatible with what he knows in the state of affairs described by μ_2, then evidently the same relation obtains between the states of affairs described by μ_3 and μ_1. In other words, it seems reasonable to adopt the following condition:

(C.trans)   If μ_2 is an alternative to μ_1 and μ_3 to μ_2, both with respect to one and the same a, then μ_3 is an alternative to μ_1 with respect to a.

There is no need, however, to adopt (C.trans) in addition to the conditions above; this condition does not in any way strengthen them. Adopting or rejecting (C.trans) does not affect the notion of defensibility at all. In this sense (C. trans) is a consequence of the other conditions.

In order to show this, let us call a member μ_2 of a model system Ω *accessible* from another member μ_1 of Ω (with respect to a) if and only if we can reach μ_2 from μ_1 in a finite number of steps each of which takes us from a model set to one of its alternatives (with respect to a).[4] Given a model system Ω which satisfies all the old conditions except, perhaps, (C.KK*), we may transform it by stipulating that μ_2 is an alternative to μ_1 (with respect to a) in the new set of sets Φ if and only if μ_2 is accessible from μ_1 (with respect to a) in Ω. (The members of Φ are those of Ω.) It is easy to verify that Φ really is a model system provided that Ω satisfies the condition (C.KK*). It is obvious that Φ satisfies the condition (C.trans).

Conversely, (C. trans) may be used to replace one of the old conditions, namely, (C.KK*)—as distinguished from (C.K*). In order to see this, let us assume that we are given a model system Ω which satisfies all the old conditions except (C.KK*) and which satisfies (C. trans). Then we may modify this Ω as follows: To each member μ of Ω we adjoin all the formulas "$K_a p$" such that "$K_a p$" ϵ λ for some member λ of Ω to which μ is an alternative with respect to a. It is not very difficult to verify that the result is a model system which satisfied all the conditions above, including (C.KK*).

---

[4] The relation of accessibility, in short, is what the logicians call the ancestral of the relation of alternativeness.

Model Sets and Systems

These observations are not without interest. What they show is, in effect, that the conditions (C.trans) and (C.KK*) are equivalent as far as the notion of defensibility is concerned. (It goes without saying that the same is true of our other basic notions, for they are defined in terms of defensibility.) Whatever evidence there is for one of the conditions may therefore be used to support the other one, too. This is important because (C.KK*) is the subtlest of our conditions, and perhaps less obvious than the others. What we have seen shows that everything which may be said in favor of (C.trans) also counts as an argument for (C.KK*).

Further support for the critical condition (C.KK*) may be obtained by means of the connection between the (C) conditions and the (A) rules which was mentioned above. This connection is such that (C.KK*) together with (C.P*) corresponds to those instances of (A.PKK*) in which $k \geqq 1$. Hence whatever intuitiveness (A.PKK*) has automatically adds to the credit of (C.KK*).

Summing up our discussion of the different ways of formulating our conditions, we may list these ways in so far as the conditions pertaining to the notion of knowledge are concerned. The most important ways are the following combinations of conditions, added to (C.P*), (C.~K), and (C.~P):

(C.K) and (C.KK*);
(C.K), (C.K*), and (C.trans);
(C.refl), (C.K*), and (C.trans);
(C.refl), (C.K*), and (C.KK*).

Unless there are indications to the contrary, we shall in the sequel confine our attention to the first two combinations, that is, disregard the condition (C.refl).

3.5. *The notion of belief*. We may discuss the notion of belief in much the same way as the notion of knowledge has just been discussed. I shall not bother the reader with the details; most of the argument would consist in retracing our steps anyway in a slightly different notation. Whoever is interested in the subject may easily convince himself that it is possible to replace '*K*' by '*B*' and '*P*' by '*C*' in most of the conditions given above. The resulting conditions will be called, in a self-explanatory terminology, (C.C*), instead of (C.P*), (C.BB*), instead of (C.KK*), and so on.

However, there is one conspicuous exception: the condition (C.K) does not have any "doxastic" counterpart. (Cf. *The Oxford English Dictionary* on "doxastic": "of, pertaining to, or depending on opinion.") That it does not is indeed perfectly obvious. What (C.K) amounts to, intuitively, is that whatever is known has to be true. There is no reason why what is believed should be true.

Another way of putting the same point is to say that (C.refl) fails to have any doxastic counterpart. The only trace of a counterpart to (C.K) or (C.refl) for the notion of belief is the doxastic counterpart of the weaker condition (C.k*). In fact, a moment's reflection promptly shows that the condition (C.b*) is indeed valid.

Although there is no counterpart to (C.K) present, it is easy to see that (C.BB*) and (C.trans) do the same job, exactly as (C.KK*) and (C.trans) did. Indeed, the argument which was outlined above as a proof of the latter fact may be adapted to prove the former one.

These considerations recommend us the following combinations of conditions (added to (C.C*), (C.∼B), and (C.∼C)):

(C.b*), (C.B*), and (C.BB*);
(C.b*), (C.B*), and (C.trans).

The only difference between the notions of knowledge and belief which we have found so far is the failure of (C.B) in contradistinction to (C.K)—except in the rudimentary form (C.b*).

48

This difference is in itself perfectly trivial; so trivial, indeed, that it may seem to have no deeper interest. It is far from trivial, however, that this single difference between the respective logics of knowledge and belief serves to explain (together with the properties which they have in common) many subtle divergencies in the logical behavior of the two notions. Cases in point are found in sections 4.3 and 4.14 below.

3.6. *Knowledge and belief combined.* We may also deal with sets of sentences which contain both the verb *know* and the verb *believe* in the same way we have dealt with sentences containing only one of them. Prima facie this task may seem easier than it is, for it may seem that all the conditions which were formulated above continue to hold without any changes. Why should the presence of one of the notions of knowledge and of belief affect the behavior of the other?

In fact, the matter is not as simple as that. It is not at all obvious that the alternatives with which such "epistemic" conditions as (C.P*), (C.K*), and (C.KK*) deal are also alternatives of the kind with which such "doxastic" conditions as (C.C*), (C.B*), (C.BB*), and (C.b*) deal. The converse relation is not obvious, either. In fact, the two kinds of alternatives have to be distinguished from each other. In the sequel, alternatives of the first kind will be called *epistemic alternatives*, and alternatives of the second kind will be called *doxastic alternatives*. In the epistemic conditions of sections 3.2–3.4 we shall from now on read "epistemic alternative" instead of "alternative" *simpliciter;* and in the doxastic conditions introduced in section 3.5 we shall from now on read "doxastic alternative" instead of "alternative" *simpliciter*. It is easily seen that some of the conditions which hold for epistemic alternatives fail to hold for doxastic alternatives. An obvious case in point is (C.refl).

The question we have to ask is, therefore: Which epistemic

conditions can be extended to hold also for doxastic alternatives, and which doxastic conditions can be extended to hold also for epistemic alternatives? The principal candidates are the following (putative) conditions:

(C.KK*dox) If "$K_a q$" ϵ μ and if μ* is a doxastic alternative to μ (with respect to a) in some model system, then "$K_a q$" ϵ μ*.

(C.K*dox) If "$K_a q$" ϵ μ and if μ* is a doxastic alternative to μ (with respect to a) in some model system, then q ϵ μ*.

(C.BB*ep) If "$B_a q$" ϵ μ and if μ* is an epistemic alternative to μ (with respect to a) in some model system, then "$B_a q$" ϵ μ*.

(C.B*ep) If "$B_a q$" ϵ μ and if μ* is an epistemic alternative to μ (with respect to a) in some model system, then q ϵ μ*.

Of these putative conditions, the fourth is clearly inadmissible, and the second is a consequence of the first. The first, in turn, is easily seen to be equivalent (as far as the notion of defensibility is concerned) to the following condition:

(C.KB) If "$K_a q$" ϵ μ, then "$B_a K_a q$" ϵ μ.

This may be expressed by saying that whenever one knows something, one believes that one knows it. But the intuitive idea behind (C.KB) and (C.KK*dox) is simpler still. In the sequel we shall see that, in a sense, whenever one knows something, one knows that one knows it. Hence it suffices for (C.KB) to assume that whatever one *knows* one also *believes*. This seems to be a reasonable assumption indeed. We have to proceed with caution here, however, keeping in mind the qualifications which were made in sections 2.6 to 2.10. It is indeed reasonable to assume that whatever one *actively* knows one also *actively* believes. But something more is required to justify (C.KB); what it really says is that whatever follows logically from what one knows also is a part of what one would believe if one would pursue the implications of one's beliefs far enough. But if I can show to you by a logical argument that q follows from what you know, then it is eminently unreasonable for you to say that you do not believe that q. Saying this would be indefensible in the very sense which we have sought to catch by our conditions and rules. For this reason, (C.KB) and therefore also (C.KK*dox) is an acceptable condition.

If we choose our other conditions in a suitable way, these conditions may even be simplified. Let us suppose that we use (C.P*), (C.K), and (C.KK*) but do not use any other epistemic conditions. Of these conditions the two first ones do not depend in any way on the question whether doxastic alternatives are also epistemic alternatives; and we just saw that the third one continues to hold even if we give an affirmative answer. Hence, under this combination of epistemic conditions (C.KK*dox) and (C.KB) can be reformulated as follows:

(C.dox)   Every doxastic alternative is also an epistemic alternative (with respect to the same free individual symbol).

3.7.   *Knowing that one believes.*   What, then, about (C.BB*ep)? It is easily seen that this condition is equivalent to the following condition (in so far as the notion of defensibility is concerned):

(C.BK)   If "$B_a q$" ϵ μ, then "$K_a B_a q$" ϵ μ.

In other words, (C.BB*ep) requires that whenever one believes something one knows that one believes it. Since (C.BK) would only be used to define the notion of indefensibility, it suffices in fact to require less; it suffices to require that whenever somebody —say the person referred to by a—is said to believe something, it must be defensible for the same speaker to add: "and *a* knows that he believes it." This sounds plausible enough. Is it not always possible for a believer to be (or at least to become) aware of his belief?

Yet we must resist the temptation to accept (C.BB*ep). Accepting this condition would force us to transfer "$B_a q$" from a model set—say μ—to its epistemic alternatives (with respect to *a*). What kind of states of affairs do these alternatives describe? Since we may transfer "$K_a p$" from μ to its epistemic alternatives (with respect to the term *a*), they describe states of affairs *in which the person referred to by this term knows at least as much as he does in the state of affairs described by μ*. Among these states there are usually some in which he would know more than he knows in μ. Now it is certainly possible that one should know more than one now does and at the same time should have fewer beliefs than one now has. In fact, it is very likely that one would have given up some of one's beliefs if one had more information. But such giving up of beliefs is just what is forbidden by (C.BB*ep).[5]

Hence (C.BB*ep) and (C.BK) are acceptable only when an unrealistically high standard of defensibility is imposed on one's beliefs. These conditions would make it (logically) indefensible to suppose that anyone would have given up any of his present beliefs if he had more information than he now has. And this is clearly too stringent a demand.

This conclusion can be reinforced by considering some of the

---

[5] It may be useful to remember that for us the primary sense of "I know that *p*" is the one in which it is roughly equivalent to "*p*, and no amount of further information would have made any difference to my saying so." Clearly, in this sense one knows that one believes something only if no amount of further information would have led one to give up one's belief.

consequences of (C.BK). By its means we could "prove," among other things, that the following sentence is self-sustaining:

"$B_a p \supset K_a P_a p$."

However, there does not seem to be any reason why one can believe only things which are known to be possible (according to what one knows). Therefore (C.BK) has to be rejected.

3.8. *The argument from introspection.* Why, then, are we tempted to assume (C.BK)? The temptation clearly comes from what I shall call an *argument from introspection.* It may seem that a mind cannot help being aware of its own states, among which there are the states of knowledge and of belief. At the very least, it seems impossible to doubt that a mind can always become aware of its own states. If I actively believe something, it might be said, surely I must be able to recognize that I do. What could there be preventing me from knowing my own mind? On what authority could anyone say that I do not know what I myself believe?

I do not want to deny that there are senses in which one's believing something implies knowing that one believes it (for one such sense, see section 4.15). It seems to me, however, that such senses are analyzable in terms of, and secondary in relation to, the sense(s) of knowledge and belief which we have been considering so far and which do not satisfy (C.BK).

Although the intimations of the argument from introspection are not without substance, they are entirely fallacious when taken at their face value. This is betrayed, among other things, by the fact that they prove far too much. If they are right, clearly they must work both ways. If I can find out by searching my mind what I know or what I believe, I must similarly be able to find out what I do not know or what I do not believe.

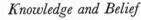

(This has in effect been claimed by some people who rely on introspective arguments.) In other words, it ought to follow, *inter alia*, that whenever I do not know something, I virtually know that I do not know it. In still other words, the following condition could be justified by an argument from introspection:

(C.PK) If "$P_a p$" ε μ, then "$K_a P_a p$" ε μ.

The consequences of this principle, however, are obviously wrong. By its means (together with certain intuitively acceptable principles) we could, for example, show that the following sentence is self-sustaining:

(13) "$p \supset K_a P_a p$."

An argument to this effect might run as follows: Suppose the contrary, that is, suppose that

(14) p ε μ ε Ω

and that

(15) "$\sim K_a P_a p$" ε μ ε Ω

for some model system Ω. Then clearly we must be able to adjoin either "$K_a \sim p$" or else "$\sim K_a \sim p$" (and therefore "$P_a p$," by (C.$\sim$K)) to μ without destroying its defensibility. The former adjunction leads to a violation of (C.$\sim$) because of (C.K) and (14). The latter adjunction would give us

"$P_a p$" ε μ

and therefore

(16) "$K_a P_a p$" ε μ by (C.PK).

Here (15) and (16) violate (C.$\sim$), demonstrating the falsity of our counterassumption.

It is perfectly obvious, however, that (13) is not acceptable.

It is not true that everybody could come to know the possibility of any fact whatsoever simply by following the consequences of what he already knows. (Some of us might, as far as logic is concerned, know nothing at all that would be relevant to the possibility of some particular p.) Therefore (C.PK) has to be rejected.

In view of the fallaciousness of the arguments from introspection it is important to realize that none of the conditions or rules we have adopted is based on them. The arguments we gave for them were all concerned with the circumstances in which a set of explicitly made statements could reasonably be said to be defensible. No reference was made to what one can know by searching one's mind. For instance, the condition (C.KK*), which is perhaps the least obvious of our conditions, should not be defended in terms of introspection. The fact that it can be defended by defending the rule (A.PKK*)—see section 2.2—shows that it is based on what might perhaps be called the quasi-performatory aspect of the verb *know*. What the rule (and therefore the condition) requires is that by saying "I know that p" one makes a commitment stronger than one made by making a simple assertion; one proposes (it is a part of one's proposition) to stick to this statement no matter what further information one expects to receive. This is what is involved in the requirement that under the epistemic alternatives to a given state of affairs one is assumed to know at least as much as he knew originally.

One reason why it is important to realize that (C.KK*) does not turn on an argument from introspection is the fact, later to be discussed, that it gives rise to conclusions which have been interpreted, and defended, in introspective terms. (See Chapter Five.) We shall see that these conclusions can be defended in an entirely different way.

3.9. *Knowledge, belief, and introspection.* Here a critic might try to turn the tables on us, blaming the failure of the arguments from introspection on our approach and not on the arguments themselves. It is impossible to make sense of the arguments by our methods, he might allege. The conditions into which we are trying to catch the logic of knowledge and belief are in terms of certain alternatives to a given state of affairs. Roughly speaking, these alternatives are possible states of affairs in which a certain person knows at least as much as—and usually even more than—he knows in the given state. In short, we are concerned with the different possibilities there are for somebody to gain further information. Now it is characteristic of the introspective knowledge we have of our own mental states that there is no room for further information. If something can only be known to me by introspection, then almost *per definitionem* I know all there is to be known about it; the notion of having further evidence becomes empty. Thus it is hopeless, a critic may suggest, to try to treat knowledge about the mental states of knowing and of believing by means of our conditions, for that would mean assimilating it to "ordinary" knowledge about the "external" world, which has different logical properties.

I shall not criticize this line of thought nor the notion of knowledge by introspection. The logic of introspection is likely to have its peculiarities. I want, however, to deny the applicability of the argument just given, whether correct or not, to the case at hand. I want to deny that knowledge and belief are mental states which can be recognized by introspection. Of course, this is a point which has been made again and again in recent discussion. I shall not give any direct arguments for it here. I shall defend it only by showing how the tendency to psychologize knowledge and belief can largely be accounted for, and disposed of. There is no need to assume that knowledge and belief are states of mind recognizable by introspection in order to understand why people have been tempted to assume that knowledge and belief are, in Ryle's word, *self-intimating*, that is, to assume that whenever one knows or believes something one knows that one does, and that whenever one does not know or believe something one knows that one does not. In fact, such an account can be based on the rules and conditions which we have already set up and which do not in any way turn on treating knowledge and belief as mental states. As was already indicated, in Chapter Five we shall see that certain conclusions which have been defended on introspective grounds admit of a different kind of defense. In Chapter Four (see especially section 4.15), we shall see that there are senses, secondary in relation to the senses explicated by our rules and conditions, in which knowledge and belief may indeed be said to be self-intimating. In sections 4.15 and 4.19 I shall call attention to certain features of the logic of knowledge and belief which may have been instrumental in leading people to connect the idea of knowledge about one's own knowledge and about one's own beliefs with introspection. In this way, certain prima-facie reasons for taking knowledge and belief to be introspectively recognizable states of mind will be (partly) explained away.

3.10.   *The self-sustenance of implications*.   In order to simplify certain types of argument it may be pointed out that a material implication "$p \supset q$" is self-sustaining if and only if the set $\{p,$ "$\sim q$"$\}$ is indefensible. This follows very easily from the definition of ' $\supset$ ' in terms of the other propositional connectives, together with those conditions which pertain to these connectives. This observation will facilitate proving virtual implications. (It was already tacitly used above in section 3.8.)

3.11.   *Reductive arguments as abortive constructions of counterexamples*.
It may be pointed out that the arguments which can be carried

out by means of the (C) conditions admit of an intuitive interpretation. In this work every proof of the fact that a statement p is self-sustaining may be thought of as an abortive attempt to describe a state of affairs (together with the requisite alternatives) in which "$\sim p$" would be true. Every proof of the indefensibility of a statement q may be interpreted as an abortive attempt to describe a state of affairs in which q would hold true; and every proof of the fact that a statement p implies epistemically another statement q is, intuitively speaking, an abortive attempt to describe consistently a state of affairs (with alternatives) in which p would be true but q false.

All these proofs are, accordingly, proofs by *reductio ad absurdum*. They start from the assumption that a certain set of sentences is defensible, that is, imbeddable in a member of a model system, and proceed to deduce a contradiction from this assumption. The contradiction completes the reductive proof, thus showing that the original set was in reality indefensible. In order to give a sample of such proofs, I shall show that "$K_a p$ & $K_a q$" virtually implies "$K_a(p \text{ & } q)$." A counterexample would be constituted by a model system Ω such that for some $\mu \ \epsilon \ \Omega$

$$\text{"}K_a p \text{ & } K_a q\text{"} \ \ \epsilon \ \ \mu \qquad \text{(first assumption)}$$

and

$$\text{"}\sim K_a(p \text{ & } q)\text{"} \ \ \epsilon \ \ \mu \qquad \text{(second assumption)}.$$

The reductive argument may proceed as follows: From the second assumption we obtain by (C.$\sim$K)

$$\text{"}P_a \sim (p \text{ & } q)\text{"} \ \ \epsilon \ \ \mu$$

and therefore by (C.P*)

$$(17) \quad \text{"}\sim(p \text{ & } q)\text{"} \ \ \epsilon \ \ \mu^* \qquad \text{(for some alternative } \mu^* \text{ to } \mu \text{ with respect to } a).$$

From the first assumption it follows by (C.&) that

$$\text{``}K_a p\text{''} \quad \epsilon \quad \mu$$

and

$$\text{``}K_a q\text{''} \quad \epsilon \quad \mu,$$

hence by (C.K*)

(18) $p \quad \epsilon \quad \mu^*$

and

(19) $q \quad \epsilon \quad \mu^*.$

From (17) it follows by (C.~&) that either

$$\text{``}\sim p\text{''} \quad \epsilon \quad \mu^*$$

or

$$\text{``}\sim q\text{''} \quad \epsilon \quad \mu^*.$$

However, the first possibility contradicts (18) and the second contradicts (19). This contradiction shows that the proposed counterexample is impossible and that the virtual implication in question really holds.

In proofs of this kind, the following sentences may be shown to be interchangeable even when they occur as parts of more comprehensive sentences: "$\sim(p$ & $q)$" and "$(\sim p$ v $\sim q)$"; "$\sim(p$ v $q)$" and "$(\sim p$ & $\sim q)$"; "$\sim\sim p$" and p; "$\sim K_a p$" and "$P_a\sim p$"; "$\sim P_a p$" and "$K_a\sim p$"; "$\sim B_a p$" and "$C_a\sim p$"; "$\sim C_a p$" and "$B_a\sim p$."

Four

Problems, Theorems, and Definitions

4.1. *Knowing that others know.* The semiformal apparatus which was built in the first three chapters of this essay may be put to test by applying it to the study of the various uses which the verbs "know" and "believe" actually have or might have. I shall endeavor to show, by discussing a few such uses, that the conditions we formulated and decided to accept in Chapter Three really catch some of the basic logic of knowledge and belief.

To begin with, it may be pointed out that our symbolism allows for an iteration of the verbs "to know" and "to believe" in one and the same sentence. In other words, our apparatus enables us to discuss such forms of words as "I know that he does not know" or "You know that I know." For instance, it may be proved that the following statement is self-sustaining:

(20)   "$K_a K_b p \supset K_a p$."

This may be proved by using the observations made in sections 3.10 and 3.11 above. The proof is a reductive one: we assume that for some model system Ω and for some $\mu \ \epsilon \ \Omega$ we have

(21)   "$K_a K_b p$" ϵ μ

and

(22)   "$\sim K_a p$" ϵ μ;

and we proceed to deduce consequences from this assumption. The deduction may have the following look:

(23)   "$P_a \sim p$" ϵ μ from (22) by (C.$\sim$K);
(24)   "$\sim p$" ϵ μ^* from (23) by (C.P*); here μ^* is an alternative to μ with respect to a in Ω;
(25)   "$K_b p$" ϵ μ^* from (21) by (C.K*);
(26) p ϵ μ^* from (25) by (C.K).

Here (24) and (26) contradict (C.$\sim$), completing our reductive argument and thereby proving that (20) really is self-sustaining.

4.2.   *The transmissibility of knowledge.*   This example may not be entirely devoid of philosophical interest. What it shows is, in effect, that knowledge is transmissible. If I know that you know that p is true, I virtually know myself that p is true. Hence, if you tell me that you know that p is true, I cannot (defensibly) deny that I know myself whether p is true without indicating that I do not wholly trust you (your judgment or your sincerity). This serves to explain why, and in what sense, "where someone has said to me 'I know,' I am entitled to say *I* know too, at second hand." The late Professor J. L. Austin, to whom the quoted sentence is due, has offered a different explanation of the transmissibility.[1] His is based on a comparison of the utter-

---

[1] See "Other Minds," *Proceedings of the Aristotelian Society*, Sup. Vol. XX (1946), 148–187; reprinted in *Logic and Language*, sec. ser., ed. by Antony Flew (Oxford, 1953), pp. 129-158, especially p. 144.

ance "I know" with the utterance "I promise." The right to say the first carries over in the same way, Austin suggests, as the right to say the second. "If someone has promised me to do A, then I am entitled to rely on it, and can myself make promises on the strength of it"; and similarly, according to Austin, "the right to say 'I know' is transmissible, in the sort of way that other authority is transmissible."

I am not sure that Austin is here right about the transmissibility of the right to make promises, and in any case it seems to me that the analogy in question is rather vague. It may therefore be of interest to note that the transmissibility of the right to say "I know" admits of a different explanation which makes no use of Austin's comparison.

A reader who is interested in comparing the two explanations may take a look at the other ways in which knowledge may be transmitted, in addition to saying "I know." For instance, let us suppose that you say to me, apropos of Dr. N. N.: "He now knows that he will get the job he has been considered for"; and let us suppose further that a third person subsequently asks me: "Do you happen to know whether Dr. N. N. will get the job he has been considered for?" If I trust you intellectually and morally, I shall naturally answer that I do know. (Of course, if I do not trust you, I shall hesitate to say this; but in that case I should hesitate even if you had said "I know.") The explanation sketched above obviously works here, for nothing was presupposed as to what *a* and *b* are in (20), whereas an explanation which is based on the authorizing character of "I know" has to be modified at least in order to cover this case. But is the present case really so different from one in which you say "I know"?

4.3. *Knowledge and belief compared with respect to transmissibility.*
Be this as it may, it is worth while to observe that no argument

like (20)–(26) can be carried out in terms of belief instead of knowledge. Since there is no analogue to (C.K) for 'B,' the step from (25) to (26) becomes inadmissible when 'K' is replaced by 'B.' Hence the argument above fails, and it may be shown that there is no way of restoring it so that it would show that

(27)   "$B_a B_b p \supset B_a p$"

is self-sustaining. (It is not.)

In view of the intuitive meaning of (27) this is not at all surprising, for beliefs are not transmissible in the way knowledge is. But it is interesting to note that this difference between the notions of knowledge and belief is explainable in terms of the trivial difference we saw obtaining between them, namely, in terms of the absence of any doxastic analogue to (C.K).

4.4.   *The difficulty of merely believing that you know.* The transition from "I know that p" as uttered by you to the same form of words as uttered by me is nevertheless a little bit trickier than we have indicated so far. The transition is not justified merely by the fact that I *believe* you; I have to *trust* you in a sense stronger than simple belief. That I believe you is expressed by the sentence

"I believe that you know that p."

This sentence does not virtually imply "I know that p." Hence there is an intermediate stage between your saying, justifiably, "I know," and my saying, justifiably, "*I* know," namely, my saying that I merely believe that you know but that I do not know myself. You may have the evidence but as long as you have not given it to me, I do not "really" know. An important part of the explanation of why and how knowledge is transmitted lies in the fact that, although there is an intermediate stage of the kind explained, it is curiously difficult to stop at. This difficulty seems to explain why it is tempting to go directly from your "I know" statement to mine.

In order to formulate the reason for the difficulty, we need certain notions which arise naturally from a discussion of Moore's problem. The rest of this chapter will be devoted to this problem and to some related problems.

4.5. *Moore's problem of saying and disbelieving.* Most of the earlier students of Moore's problem [2] have claimed that the paradoxical sentence

(8) "*p* but I do not believe that *p*"

is not self-contradictory. Such a view may itself strike one as paradoxical. It is not difficult, as demonstrated by Tennesen,[3] to prompt people into calling (8) self-contradictory in so many

---

[2] See G. E. Moore, *Ethics* (London, 1912), p. 125, reset ed. (London, 1947), p. 78; G. E. Moore, "A Reply to My Critics," in *The Philosophy of G. E. Moore*, ed. by P. A. Schilpp (Evanston, Ill., 1942), especially pp. 541–543; G. E. Moore, "Russell's 'Theory of Descriptions,'" in *The Philosophy of Bertrand Russell*, ed. by P. A. Schilpp (Evanston, Ill., 1944), pp. 177–225, especially pp. 203–204; reprinted in G. E. Moore, *Philosophical Papers* (London, 1959), pp. 151–195, especially pp. 175–176; A. M. MacIver, "Some Questions about 'Know' and 'Think,'" *Analysis*, V (1938), 43–50; reprinted in *Philosophy and Analysis*, ed. by Margaret MacDonald (Oxford, 1954), pp. 88–95; A. Duncan-Jones, "Further Questions about 'Know' and 'Think,'" *Analysis*, V (1938), 74–83; reprinted in *Philosophy and Analysis*, pp. 96–106; A. M. MacIver, "Reply to Duncan-Jones," *Analysis*, V (1938), 95–97; reprinted in *Philosophy and Analysis*, pp. 106–108; Max Black, "Saying and Disbelieving," *Analysis*, XIII (1952), 25–33; reprinted in *Philosophy and Analysis*, pp. 109–119; also reprinted in Max Black, *Problems of Analysis* (Ithaca, N.Y., 1954), pp. 46–57; Ludwig Wittgenstein, *Philosophische Untersuchungen* (Oxford, 1953), II, x; cf. also Norman Malcolm, *Ludwig Wittgenstein: A Memoir* (Oxford, 1958), pp. 66–67; Y. Bar-Hillel, "Analysis of 'Correct' Language," *Mind*, N.S. LV (1946), 328–340; Y. Bar-Hillel, "Indexical Expressions," *Mind*, N.S. LXIII (1954), 359–379.

[3] See Herman Tennessen, "Logical Oddities and Locutional Scarcities," *Synthese*, XI (1959), 369–388, especially pp. 378–379.

words. In spite of attempts to maintain the contrary, most people would probably admit there is something *logically* very queer about (8).

The consistency of our sentence (8) has been maintained by claiming that the proposition expressed by (8) is consistent. The notion of proposition used here is far from clear, however. That it easily gives rise to arguments which are quite unreliable is demonstrated by Duncan-Jones's able criticism of MacIver. I shall dispense with it altogether.

It does not matter, of course, what a sentence is called as long as we know what the facts are and how they are to be explained. Those who have denied that (8) is self-contradictory have clearly been impressed by certain differences between (8) and such typically self-contradictory sentences as are studied in elementary logic. There the self-contradictoriness of a sentence like "p & $\sim p$" is not removed by a mere change of person, in contradistinction to the fact that a change of person turns (8) into the perfectly natural sentence

(28)   "p but he does not believe that p."

In general, most sentences of the form

(8)(a)   "p but a does not believe that p"

are obviously quite all right.

Similarly a change of tense removes the absurdity of (8), as witnessed by such a sentence as

(29)   "He was at home but I did not believe it."

An unnaturalness removable in this way seems rather different from plain self-contradiction. Furthermore (8) is all right if prefixed by such a word as "suppose":

"Suppose that this mushroom is poisonous but I do not believe it"

65

is intelligible, whereas "suppose that p and $\sim p$" is as wrong logically as "p & $\sim p$" (except in certain circumstances such as a proof by a *reductio ad absurdum*).

Such peculiarities of (8) naturally lead one to emphasize the difference between the absurdity of (8) and that of typical self-contradictions. The view that (8) is not self-contradictory may be taken to mean that this gulf is unbridgeable, that there is no way of reducing (8) to the contradictions of elementary logic.

In a way, I am myself in a similar position. Clearly (8) is not indefensible according to the criteria I have set up so far. Hence I shall have to look for a different explanation of its absurdity.

But could not the defensibility of (8) according to my criteria be perhaps due rather to the fact that the criteria are not strong enough? I do not think so. I shall argue that the absurdity of (8) can be explained without strengthening our criteria. A comparison between (8) and (28) or (8)(a) shows that the new criteria of indefensibility which would be needed must give a special role to the first-person singular pronoun "I." For the corresponding sentences in the other persons are not absurd (except perhaps those in the first person plural). An explanation that avoids such a complication seems preferable to additional criteria. I shall suggest a reason for the absurdity which does not presuppose any changes in the criteria of defensibility and indefensibility. My explanation also serves to account for the differences between (8) and the typical contradictions of elementary logic. But it is not the case that my explanation is preferable to an attempt to elaborate the criteria of indefensibility in order to account for the absurdity of (8) only because of its economy; later we shall see that any attempt to account for (8) in terms of the peculiarities of first-person pronouns is in principle misguided. (See section 4.8.)

Problems and Definitions

4.6. *Our solution.* The explanation I shall offer turns on the fact that, although (8) is defensible, the closely related form of words

> (30) "I believe that the case is as follows: p but I do not believe that p."

is *in*defensible. The explanation is as follows: What is violated by uttering (8) is not logical consistency (defensibility) but rather the general presumption that the speaker believes or at least can conceivably believe what he says. This presumption amounts to requiring that (30) is either defensible or, if indefensible, so complicated that its indefensibility is not felt (however inarticulately) by the speaker. Now the latter alternative is ruled out by the simplicity of (8) and by the consequent intuitiveness of what (30) expresses. The former alternative is ruled out by the indefensibility of (30). In short, the gist of Moore's paradox may be said (somewhat elliptically) to lie in the fact that (8) is necessarily *unbelievable* by the speaker.

From this point of view, it is understood at once why the result of changing the person in (8) is not absurd. For what is expected when somebody utters

> (8)(a) "p but a does not believe that p"

(where a is neither the pronoun "I" nor the speaker's own name) is similarly that it is possible for him to believe what he says, that is, it would be defensible for him to say:

> (30)(a) "I believe that the case is as follows: p but a does not believe that p."

This sentence is of the form

> (30)(a)* "$B_b(p \;\&\; \sim B_a p)$"

while (30) is of the form

(30)* "$B_a(p$ & $\sim B_a p)$."

As we shall see, (30)(a)* is defensible—unless a is identical with b—but (30)* indefensible.

In a sense, therefore, the paradoxical character of (8) does not turn on the peculiarities of the first-person singular pronoun, namely, in the sense that (30)* is indefensible no matter what a is (whether a name or a personal pronoun). In another sense, of course, the absurdity of (8) is due to the fact that it is in the first person, namely, in the sense that (8) kindles the presumption that (30) is defensible whereas (8)(a) only gives rise to the presumption that (30)(a) is defensible. And statements of the general form (30)(a)* are indefensible only if $a = b$.

The fact that (30)* is indefensible no matter what a is seems to be consonant with our intuitions. For what is expressed by

(31) "a believes that the case is as follows: p but a does not believe that p"

is something which can be changed by pointing out to the person referred to by a that his beliefs are contradictory. Hence (31) is indefensible in the sense we have given to the term.[4]

We can now also understand why such a sentence as (29) is not absurd in the same way as (8). When somebody utters (29), we are normally entitled to expect that it would be defensible for him to say:

---

[4] In section 4.7 we shall see that the indefensibility of (31) turns on the condition (C.BB*), i.e., on the rule (A.CBB*). Its indefensibility is therefore subject to qualifications similar to those we found it necessary to make at the end of section 2.2: there is something wrong about (31) only on the assumption that the person referred to by a believes that he is referred to by it. If a is a description (e.g., "the next President"), this assumption may not be fulfilled.

(32) "I believe that the case is as follows: he was at home but I did not believe it"

in the same way as we should be led to expect the defensibility of (30) by the uttering of (8). In contradistinction to (30), however, (32) is clearly defensible. (We have no ways of proving its defensibility formally, for we are not dealing with the logic of tenses in this essay, but the point is obvious enough.) This serves to explain the difference between (8) and (29).

Notice, incidentally, that every instance of (30)* is indefensible no matter in what tense it is (as long as all the clauses of the sentence pertain to one and the same moment of time). For instance, however natural (29) is, it is highly paradoxical to say:

"I believed at the time that p but that I did not believe that p."

4.7. *Proof of the solution.* My main thesis still remains to be proved. By means of the normal reductive strategy the indefensibility of (30)* may be demonstrated by assuming that, on the contrary,

$$"B_a(p \ \& \ \sim B_a p)" \ \epsilon \ \mu$$

for some member μ of some model system Ω and by reducing this counterassumption *ad absurdum* as follows:

(33) $"p \ \& \ \sim B_a p" \ \epsilon \ \mu^*$ from the counterassumption by (C.b*);

(34) $"B_a(p \ \& \ \sim B_a p)" \ \epsilon \ \mu^*$ from the counterassumption by (C.BB*);

(35) $"\sim B_a p" \ \epsilon \ \mu^*$ from (33) by (C.&);

(36) $"C_a \sim p" \ \epsilon \ \mu^*$ from (35) by (C.$\sim$B);

(37) $"\sim p" \ \epsilon \ \mu^{**}$ from (36) by (C.C*);

(38) $"p \ \& \ \sim B_a p" \ \epsilon \ \mu^{**}$ from (34) by (C.B*);

(39) $p \ \epsilon \ \mu^{**}$ from (38) by (C.&).

Here (37) and (39) contradict (C.~), thus completing our reductive argument. Its shortness and simplicity justify my assumption that its force is felt, more or less inarticulately, by the speakers
of "ordinary language." Its intuitive simplicity may be enhanced
by observing that the two uses of (C.&) in the argument are
quite trivial, and that the steps (37) and (38) may in effect be
comprised into a single application of (A.CB*).

It is readily seen that the argument fails if (30)* is replaced
by (30)(a)*, for then the third model set μ^{**} mentioned in the
argument need not be an alternative to the second set with
respect to a. Consequently the step (38) becomes invalid. By
pushing the procedure to the limit, we may even find a model
system which shows that (30)(a)* is defensible.

In the argument (33)–(39) we made use of the condition
(C.BB*). Although I think that this condition is normally satisfied, it may nevertheless be interesting to observe that in a sense
our explanation of the absurdity of (8) can be made independent
of it. The explanation turns on the fact that (8) is impossible for
the speaker to believe. Instead of taking this to mean that (30)
is obviously indefensible, we may alternatively take it to mean
that the speaker could not have added "and I believe what I
just said" without making the resulting pair of statements obviously indefensible. In other words, the impossibility of believing
(8) could also be shown by demonstrating that sentences of the
following form are indefensible:

$$\text{``}(p \ \& \ \sim B_a p) \ \& \ B_a(p \ \& \ \sim B_a p)\text{.''}$$

This could be done by means of an argument which is almost
exactly like (33)–(39). The only difference is that the new argument is simpler: we could identify the sets μ and μ^*, and the
first two steps (33) and (34) could be replaced by a single application of the trivial condition (C.&). In this way, our explanation

could be made independent of (C.BB*), and the argument (33)–(39) simpler still.

4.8. *Doxastic indefensibility.*   It is instructive to try to generalize the explanation we gave of the peculiarity of (8). One way of doing so is as follows:

Let us assume that the person referred to by *a* makes a finite number of statements, that is, utters a finite number of declarative sentences p_1, p_2, p_3, . . . , p_k, on one and the same occasion. Let us assume, furthermore, that every time he refers to himself in these statements he does so by using a certain term, say *a*. Then we shall call the set $\{p_1, p_2, . . . , p_k\}$ *doxastically indefensible for the person referred to by this term to utter* if and only if the sentence

"$B_a(p_1 \& p_2 \& . . . \& p_k)$"

is indefensible *simpliciter*. The intended generalization may now be expressed by saying that the absurdity of (8) is due to the fact that it is *doxastically* indefensible for the speaker to utter (although it is not itself indefensible) and that this doxastic indefensibility is demonstrable in so simple a way it is felt by the speakers of the English language.

If (C.BB*) is satisfied, our definition of doxastic indefensibility is equivalent to the following alternative definition: The set in question is doxastically indefensible for the person referred to by *a* to utter if and only if the set obtained by adding the further sentence "$B_a(p_1 \& p_2 \& . . . \& p_k)$" is indefensible *simpliciter*. This alternative definition would often make it easier to demonstrate the doxastic indefensibility of sets of sentences. But it would also make certain sentences or sets of sentences we want to consider more complicated. For this reason, we shall normally use the original definition.

The definition of doxastic indefensibility shows that this notion constitutes a direct generalization of the puzzling properties of Moore's sentence (8). Doxastically indefensible statements (utterances)[5] might be true in the sense that the same form of words could be used by some other speaker to make a correct and true statement. (E.g., (8)(a) could be true and still doxastically indefensible for the person referred to by *a* to utter.) Doxastically indefensible statements are nevertheless impossible for the speaker to believe consistently. And this unbelievability of theirs is of a logical character; it can be seen from the very form of words the speaker is using (provided that we know how he is referring to himself). Doxastically indefensible statements are therefore *self-defeating*. By making such a statement the speaker gives his hearers all they need to overthrow his statement (to the extent of showing that he cannot consistently believe what he says). They are for the same reason *absurd* to make if the speaker is aware of their self-defeating character. It is normally impossible for the hearers to understand what such a speaker could conceivably be trying to accomplish. If the doxastically indefensible statement in question is more complicated, however, it is possible that the speaker does not realize that it is self-defeating. In such a case, the statement might not be absurd in the sense that we could perhaps see what he is trying to do. It is nevertheless self-defeating exactly in the same sense as Moore's paradoxical sentence (8).[6]

---

[5] I shall speak of doxastically indefensible *statements* although I realize that in some of the natural senses of the word such utterances do not qualify as statements. It might be argued that the notion of a statement presupposes that the speaker can possibly believe what he says (states). However, this is not the sense in which I am using the word here. If my usage is uncongenial to you, please read "putative statement" instead of "statement."

[6] Alternatively, the speaker might fail to believe that the person for whom a sentence is doxastically indefensible to utter is himself. This makes a difference to the situation because our explanations for the

Problems and Definitions

The main generalization here (over and above our original remarks on Moore's problem) consists in allowing for the possibility that the speaker (or writer) is referring to himself in a way different from using the first-person singular pronoun "I." This generalization may strike the reader as being rather unimportant. It is unusual for a speaker or writer to refer to himself in other ways. (Instances of such a usage are not unheard-of, however, as witnessed by the memoirs of Caesar and De Gaulle.) But the main interest of the generalization was not intended to lie in an increased applicability to ordinary discourse. It lies rather in the possibility of bringing in this way into a sharper focus certain features of our analysis of Moore's problem. What the feasibility of the generalization shows is that there could be puzzling statements similar to the ones made by uttering (8) even if there were no personal pronouns in our language. For the notion of doxastic indefensibility was defined without making any reference to the peculiarities of personal pronouns. The paradoxical utterances could even be analyzed in the same way we analyzed the mechanism of Moore's paradox. In this sense, the absence of first-person pronouns would make little difference to Moore's

---

absurdity of doxastically indefensible statements (say of those which are indefensible for the referent of a to make) are based on the assumption that the person in question believes that he is referred to by it. An explanation which turns on the indefensibility of $(30)^*$ is based on this assumption since the proof of the indefensibility of $(30)^*$ made use of (C.BB*). An alternative explanation in which it is required that the person referred to by a should be able to add, defensibly, "and a believes what he just said" is likewise based on the same assumption since there is nothing odd in a refusal to make such an addition as long as this refusal is merely due to the fact that the speaker does not believe that he is referred to by a.

In such cases, the act of making a doxastically indefensible statement need not be pointless. The statement in question is nevertheless vulnerable in a peculiar way: all we need to overthrow it is to find out the identity of the speaker and to point it out to him.

problem. What would be different is that we could not speak any longer of doxastically indefensible *sentences*. The notion of doxastic indefensibility was not defined, unlike the other notions we have defined so far, for *sentences* (or for sets of sentences) as much as for sets of *statements*. It does not depend solely on the forms of words uttered; it also depends on the speaker (or writer) and on the ways in which he is referring to himself. It can be defined for sets of sentences only by making it relative to a name or a pronoun occurring in the sentences in question. Where the intended speaker (or writer) is obvious, we may occasionally drop the clause "for . . . to make"; but then the identity of the speaker (or writer) has to be gathered from the context.

The main exception is the case in which the speaker refers to himself by means of the first-person singular pronoun. As soon as a sentence contains the word "I," it is obvious how the speaker is referring to himself.[7] The clause 'for the person referred to by *a* to utter' which we used in the definition of the doxastic indefensibility becomes empty when *a* = "I" and may often be omitted, for then it takes the form "for whoever happens to be speaking to utter" and means no more than "for anybody to utter." Thus we may define the notion of doxastic indefensibility for *sentences* of a certain particular kind absolutely, namely, for sentences containing the first-person singular pronoun "I," although we cannot in general define it for sentences without relativizing it.[8] The main feature, it may be said, of our discussion of Moore's paradox which turned on the peculiarities of

---

[7] For simplicity, we have assumed that the speaker does not refer to himself in more than one way. This assumption could be dispensed with if we had the notion of identity at our disposal.

[8] It is pointless to try to extend the unrelativized notion of doxastic indefensibility beyond sentences containing first-person pronouns. In the sequel we shall assume that it is defined only for these.

first-person pronouns is therefore the fact that we could carry it on in terms of sentences instead of statements. We shall soon see, however, that this fact does not exempt Moore's paradoxical sentence (8) from the peculiarities which are typical of doxastically indefensible statements.

The possibility of generalizing the paradoxical properties of (8) in the way we have done is also interesting because it shows that an attempt to explain the absurdity of (8) in the sole terms of the peculiarities of the first-person singular pronoun is necessarily misguided. Such an explanation could not serve to explain why (8)(a) is absurd for the person referred to by *a* to utter, for (8)(a) need not contain any pronouns whatsoever. Yet the reason for the absurdity of such a statement is obviously the same as the reason for the absurdity of the sentence (8).

We can now also see a reason why (8) could be said to be as good a *sentence* as (8)(a). There is in our language a general parallelism between sentences in the first person singular and similar sentences in which the speaker's name replaces the first-person pronoun. There is always at least one clear-cut way of giving a use to a sentence in the first person singular—e.g., (8) —provided that the corresponding sentences in which a name replaces the pronoun—e.g., (8)(a)—have already been given a use. All we have to do is to stipulate that the former sentence *as uttered by the person referred to by a name* (let this name be *a*) has the same use(s) as the sentence (uttered by the same person) in which *a* replaces "I." For instance, all we have to do in order to give a well-defined use to (8) is to give (8)(a) a use in the case in which *a* is the speaker's own name. If (8)(a) were always completely unproblematic when *a* is a proper name, then so would be (8). As it happens, exactly those utterances of (8)(a) are self-defeating which would be needed to make sense of any use of (8).

In this sense, (8) is quite as correct a *sentence* as (8)(a). This is reflected by the fact that in our classification it is a defensible sentence. It is also reflected by our feeling that (8), however absurd it may be to utter, somehow describes a "state of affairs" which is not impossible: it might be the case that p is true although I do not believe it.

Our feeling may perhaps be heightened (and justified) by observing that it is not strictly speaking true to say that an doxastically indefensible sentence is self-defeating for anyone to utter. If it appears from the context that I am merely contemplating a possibility, the act of uttering it may perhaps serve a purpose. (If Oliver Cromwell had said, in a moment of self-scrutiny: "By the bowels of Christ—I must believe it possible: The Scotchmen are right and I don't believe them," we could understand him.) A doxastically indefensible sentence becomes absurd only when somebody utters it so as to suggest that he believes what he says; in short, when somebody tries to *profess* what it expresses (in one of the senses of the word).

4.9. *Doxastic implication.* In terms of the notion of doxastic indefensibility we may define the notion of *doxastic implication* by saying that p implies q doxastically if and only if the set $\{p, \text{``} \sim q\text{''}\}$ is doxastically indefensible. (In this sense, p implies doxastically "I believe that p.") Furthermore, we could define the notion of doxastic self-sustenance as follows: p is doxastically self-sustaining if and only if "I do not believe that p" is indefensible. In the same way as doxastically indefensible sentences may be true but are for logical reasons unbelievable by the speaker, in the same way doxastically self-sustaining sentences are for logical reasons impossible for anybody to doubt, provided that he appreciates their logic. This interesting notion is superfluous, however. As you may have expected, a sentence can be doxastically self-sustaining only if it is self-sustaining *simpliciter*.

Problems and Definitions

4.10. *The performatoriness of doxastic indefensibility.* Sentences which are doxastically indefensible but not indefensible *simpliciter* have interesting features in common, most of which are illustrated by Moore's paradoxical sentence (8). Suppose that p is doxastically indefensible for the person referred to by a to utter but not indefensible *simpliciter*, say the sentence "r but a does not believe it." Then p is perfectly all right as a sentence; it becomes absurd only when it is uttered by a particular person. Suppose, further, that q is like p except that the first-person singular pronoun "I" plays the role a played in p, for example, the sentence "r but I don't believe it." In the same way as p becomes absurd only when a certain particular person utters it, it may be said that q is also all right as such. It becomes strange only when somebody (anybody) actually tries to profess what it expresses. (He may profess it to others, that is, he may utter it so as to make others think he believes it, or he may try to "say it in his heart" in the Biblical sense of believing it himself.) By their very definition, doxastically indefensible sentences are not so much wrong per se as self-defeating *for anybody to utter.* Even though the use of first-person pronouns makes it possible for us to speak of indefensible sentences and not merely of indefensible statements, the logical parentage of this "absolute" notion of doxastic indefensibility is thus betrayed by the fact that their self-defeating character manifests itself only when they are assertively uttered or otherwise professed. In a sense, therefore, the absurdity of doxastically indefensible sentences is of *performatory character;* it is due to doing something rather than to the means (to the sentence) which is employed for the purpose. One finds it more natural to say that uttering the sentence p doxastically implies "I believe that p" than to say that the former sentence "by itself" doxastically implies the latter.

This, of course, is but a reflection of the logical facts we have been discussing. Another reflection is the peculiar difficulty one encounters when trying to express the reason for the strangeness of doxastically indefensible sentences without using,[9] overtly or covertly, first-person pronouns. For instance, I shall argue (see section 4.20) that the absurdity of (8) cannot be accounted for by saying, as Moore has done, that whoever says something is likely to believe what he says, in spite of the fact that this might look like the most straightforward generalization of the insight that p implies doxastically "I believe that p." In a certain sense, doxastic implications are not generalizable. Each of us can formulate one "for himself," so to speak; but there is no way of dispensing with the first-person pronoun "I" except by speaking of statements (speech-acts) and not only of sentences (forms of words).

4.11. *An analogue to Moore's problem for the notion of knowledge.* The crucial argument (33)–(39) carries through without any changes if '*B*' is replaced by '*K*' and '*C*' by '*P*.' Hence we also obtain an explanation why the form of words

(9) "p but I do not know whether p"

is often somewhat awkward although it is not itself indefensible.[10] The explanation may run as follows: When somebody makes a statement—say, utters the sentence q—we are normally led to expect that he can conceivably know that what he is saying is true or that he is at least not depriving himself of this possibility by the very form of words he is using. Whatever absurdity there is about (9) is due to the fact that in the case $q =$ "p but I do

---

[9] More accurately, using or mentioning.

[10] The significance of (9) may perhaps be saved by taking it to mean the same as

(47) "I believe that p but I do not know it."

But then the question becomes: Why is (47) a much more natural thing to say than (9)?

not know whether p" this expectation is not fulfilled, for what we just observed shows, in effect, that it is indefensible to say

(40)   "I know that the case is as follows: p but I do not know whether p."

This is not quite so, for the transcription of (40) into our symbolic notation is not

(41)   "$K_a(p \ \& \ \sim K_a p)$"

which was just seen to be indefensible, but rather

(40)*   "$K_a(p \ \& \ \sim K_a p \ \& \ \sim K_a \sim p)$"

as indicated by (4)*; but (40)* may be proved indefensible in the same way as (41).

In one respect the proof that (41) and (40)* are indefensible can be made simpler than the corresponding proof for (30)*. In the proof for (41) we may identify the two sets μ and μ^* in (33)–(39). Then (34) is tantamount to the counterassumption, and (33) is obtained from the counterassumption by an application of (C.K). The use of the critical condition (C.KK*) can thus be avoided altogether. Sentences of form (40)* may be dealt with similarly.

4.12.   *Epistemic indefensibility.*   The properties of (9) may be generalized in the same way as those of (8). In analogy to the definition of doxastic indefensibility given in section 4.8 we may define what it means for a set of sentences $\{p_1, p_2, \ldots, p_k\}$ to be *epistemically indefensible* for the person referred to by a to utter: it means that the sentence

"$K_a(p_1 \ \& \ p_2 \ \& \ \ldots \ \& \ p_k)$"

is indefensible *simpliciter*.

This notion of epistemic indefensibility enables us to define what it means for p to *imply q epistemically:* it means that "$(p \ \& \sim q)$" is epistemically indefensible.

Knowledge and Belief

4.13. *Applications.* Our generalization of the properties of (9) in terms of the notion of epistemic indefensibility may cover cases which have some independent interest. For instance, we may now see why

> (42) "He knows that p but I don't know it"

is sometimes (not always) a somewhat strange thing to say. The explanation consists in observing that (42) is epistemically indefensible—and that this observation can be made by means of a very simple argument.

This shows that John Hartland-Swann is, in a sense, right in saying that in every "he knows"-statement there is a suppressed or understood "I know"-statement.[11] For we have just pointed out that "he knows that p" implies epistemically "I know that p." Speaking of suppressed or understood statements is a very loose way of speaking, however, which easily leads one astray. For instance, it leads us to expect that in every "he knows whether"-statement there similarly is a tacit "I know whether"-statement. For each "he knows whether"-statement is but a disjunction of two "he knows that"-statements—see (2)*—each of which might on Hartland-Swann's principles be expected to imply the corresponding tacit "I know that"-statement. In spite of this, it is perfectly obvious that there is nothing wrong with sentences of the form

> (43) "He knows whether p although I don't."

From our point of view, this is only to be expected, for (43) is, unlike (42), epistemically defensible, as the reader is invited to verify. Furthermore, Hartland-Swann's way of putting his point seems rather too strong in that (42) may occasionally be less unnatural than his formulation suggests (cf. section 4.21).

---

[11] *An Analysis of Knowing* (London, 1958), pp. 27–28.

Problems and Definitions

The general form of (42) is

$$(42)^* \quad \text{``}(K_a p \ \& \ \sim K_b p).\text{''}$$

The fact that $(42)^*$ is epistemically indefensible for the bearer of b to utter may throw some light on the problems discussed in section 4.4. It shows that there obtains an epistemic implication between "you know that" (or "he knows that") and "I know that." For this reason, it is peculiarly difficult to stop between the two. Or perhaps I should rather say that stopping at such a point is very precarious; it would mean entertaining opinions which one cannot conceivably know to be true and which one is therefore liable to give up with further information.

We are now also in a position to qualify our discussion of the problem of translating (3) into our symbolism (section 1.7). We found that the best translation of (3) is $(3)^*$ when (3) occurs in the context of normal statement-making discourse. Even in such contexts, however, $(3)^*$ is not always a very natural translation. For if a is the first-person singular pronoun "I," then the resulting translation $(3)^*$ is tantamount to (9) and hence epistemically indefensible. Since an epistemically indefensible sentence is felt to be odd, people usually try to supply a different kind of context or else simply to understand the sentence as being equivalent to "$\sim K_a p$" and not to $(3)^*$.

We may similarly dispel an objection which may have lingered in the reader's mind since section 2.4. There we suggested that it is not impossible that somebody might be aware of something without being aware that he is aware. We also maintained that it might seem to somebody that p is the case while it does not seem to him that this is how things seem to him. These claims may strike you as being very dubious. Surely a man is not altogether consistent, you may have wanted to say, if he is aware of something without being aware that he is aware; something is wrong with him conceptually. In a sense, you are right. What is wrong with our man is that he does not recognize an epistemic implication. "I am aware that p" implies "I am aware that I am aware that p" in the sense a man who affirms the first but denies the second cannot possibly be aware that what he says is true. (That such an epistemic implication holds here follows from what was said in 4.11. There we saw that any q can be shown to imply epistemically "I know that q" without using (C.KK*). This means that a similar implication is provable for the notion of awareness although this notion does not satisfy (C.KK*).) Thus a man who is aware of something but not aware that he is aware of it cannot describe his situation without defeating his own purpose. He could not say "I am aware that p but I am not aware that I am aware of it" without making an epistemically indefensible statement. But we did not maintain in 2.4 that he can do this. We only maintained that somebody else could say *of him* "he is aware that p but is not aware that he is aware" without being inconsistent (even by implication). In other words, we did not deny the *epistemic* implication from "I am aware that p" to "I am aware that I am aware that p" but the *virtual* implication from "a is aware that p" to "a is aware that he is aware that p." I think a perceptive reader sees the great difference between the two cases.

4.14. *Knowledge and belief compared.* We have given parallel explanations of the peculiarities of (8) and (9), respectively. If there is a difference between the two cases, it is likely to be a difference in degree: (9) seems to me distinctly less strange—in so far as it is strange at all—than (8). If this is really the case, an explanation is forthcoming: other things being equal, it is less unnatural to say something one does not (and cannot) know than to say something one obviously does not (and cannot) believe.

Other differences between the notions of knowledge and belief

may also be brought out by our methods. We have seen that
(41) and (30)* are both indefensible; it may now be observed
that the closely related forms of words

$$(44) \quad ``K_a(p \ \& \ \sim B_a p)"$$

and

$$(45) \quad ``B_a(p \ \& \ \sim K_a p)"$$

are not equal in this respect. The former may be shown—by
means of (C.dox)—to be indefensible along the same lines as
(30)*, while the latter is easily seen to be defensible. A model
system which shows this might be $\Omega = \{\mu, \mu^*, \mu^{**}\}$, where the
second set is a doxastic alternative to the first as well as to itself
and the third an epistemic alternative to the second, all with
respect to a, and where $\mu = \{``B_a(p \ \& \ \sim K_a p)"\}$; $\mu^* = \{``B_a(p$
$\& \ \sim K_a p),"$ $``p \ \& \ \sim K_a p,"$ $p,$ $``\sim K_a p,"$ $``P_a \sim p"\}$; and $\mu^{**} =$
$\{``\sim p"\}$.

The defensibility of (45) squares fairly well with our intuitions.
For instance, I may perfectly well believe that (as of now) some
expected event has already happened although I have not yet
been informed of it. It is true that the form of words

(46)   "I believe that p but that I do not know whether p"

does not sound quite all right here; we are tempted to drop the
second "that" and to say instead

(47)   "I believe that p but I do not know it."

This, however, does not tell against our theory. The reason why
(46) is slightly queer lies probably just in the fact that it is more
complicated than (47). For what they express is almost exactly
the same: (46) virtually implies (47) while the latter implies the
former doxastically, as you may verify. Hence the added complexity of (46) as compared with (47) is felt to be irrelevant.
Notice, in particular, that the virtual implication means that

whoever is in a position to say (46) is already in the position to make the more straightforward statement (47).

It is instructive to compare a statement of the form (47) with one of the form (9) in its own right. The former is a perfectly natural form of words. By the principles we used to explain the peculiarity of the latter, the result of prefixing "I know that the case is as follows" to (47) should therefore be defensible. And it is in fact defensible indeed. Although (41) is an indefensible form of words,

(48) "$K_a(B_a p$ & $\sim K_a p)$"

is not, as one can easily show by exhibiting an appropriate model system. (The reader will not find any difficulties in constructing one.) Nor is

"$K_a(B_a p$ & $\sim K_a p$ & $\sim K_a \sim p)$"

indefensible. Thus we have more evidence that on our principles the line between absurd and natural forms of words goes where we naturally expect it to go. (Cf. note 10 of this chapter.)

4.15. *Introspectiveness as a symptom of an epistemic implication.* Now we may also appreciate better the temptation to assume that knowledge and belief are self-intimating or at least infallibly recognizable by introspection, to assume, in other words, that whenever we know or believe something we know (or at least *can* know, merely by reflecting on the consequences of what we do) that we know or believe, and that whenever we do not know or believe something we know (or can know) that we do not. It was already pointed out that in the most literal sense knowledge and belief are not self-intimating. For instance, "$B_a p$" does not virtually imply "$K_a B_a p$." (See section 3.7.) It is easily seen, however, that a closely related implication is valid: "I believe that p" implies *epistemically* "I know that I believe that p." The mistaken idea that "$B_a p$" should in some stronger sense imply "$K_a B_a p$" may be partly (or wholly) due to a confusion between the different implications.

Similarly, most of the other implications which would make knowledge and belief self-intimating have to be construed as epistemic implications between first-person sentences rather than virtual implications between third-person sentences. (In one case, there obtains a virtual implication; see Chapter Five.) Thus construed, they are entirely valid, as you may verify. Hence the intimations of introspection are not completely devoid of substance. But we have to be aware of the sense in which they are correct. The very fact that one has to appeal to introspection when defending an implication shows that there is something unusual about it. The necessity of making the appeal is, in the case at hand, a symptom of the fact that the implication in question is epistemic rather than virtual. Remember that a sentence —say p—which is epistemically indefensible for the person referred to by a to utter need not for this reason be *absurd* for him to utter. It is not absurd (although it may be said to be self-defeating) for a man to say "I have deceived my worst enemy" even if he really is his own worst enemy. Such a sentence becomes absurd for him to utter only when he realizes that the person whose knowledge (or belief) is being spoken of in p is himself.[12] Similarly, the absurdity of epistemically indefensible sentences in the

---

[12] In order to recognize a statement as epistemically indefensible I have to know the speaker to the extent of being able to identify him as the very same man whom his statement is about. In order to recognize an epistemic implication in the first person I likewise have to "identify myself," to discover that the man referred to is necessarily myself. No wonder, therefore, that epistemic implications (and some closely related implications) have been connected with the notion of personal identity. See Locke's *Essay concerning Human Understanding*, bk. II, ch. xxvii, sec. 11 (Fraser's ed. [Oxford, 1894], I, 448–449). Cf. *ibid.* bk. II, ch. i, sec. 12 (Fraser's ed., I, 131–132).

first person singular is due to the fact that the person whose knowledge (or belief) is being discussed necessarily is the speaker himself. The reference to introspection here amounts to little more, it seems to me, than a mythical description of this simple conceptual insight. In order to recognize an epistemic implication, I am tempted to say, one has to commit what William James called "the psychologist's fallacy": one has to identify one's standpoint "with that of a mental fact" (rather, with that of the subject whose knowledge or belief is being discussed).[13] Conversely, not recognizing an epistemic (or doxastic) implication may be due to a kind of duality, not to say duplicity, within one's own mind and therefore may sometimes have a touch of self-deception in it.

Epistemic implications are mistaken for virtual ones because people do not sufficiently appreciate the logic of first-person pronouns. One takes oneself as a paradigm without realizing what it involves. Because we can say, correctly in a sense, "I know what I know and what I believe, and what I don't," we are tempted to think that there is an equally straightforward sense in which we can say, "Everybody knows what he knows and what he believes, and what he doesn't." The interpretation, however, which made the first-person sentence valid is tied to the peculiarities of the first-person singular pronoun. A generalization enables us to get rid of the pronoun only if we insert a reference to statements as distinguished from the sentences thereby uttered. We may indeed carry out a kind of generalization by saying, for example, that it is self-defeating for anybody to *say*, whether aloud or in his heart, "*a* believes that *p* but he

[13] The fallacy is expounded in *The Principles of Psychology: The Long Course* (New York, 1890), I, 196–197. If the distinction between virtual and epistemic implications is heeded, however, James's "fallacy" need not be fallacious at all. It is not the *psychologist's* fallacy, either, in the sense that psychologists are particularly prone to commit it. It is theirs in the sense that it is fallacious only for their purposes. Cf. sec. 5.8.

does not know that he believes" when *a* refers *to the speaker*. But here it is necessary to refer to a speech- or thought-act.

But is this explanation of the temptation to think that knowledge and belief are always recognizable by introspection sufficient? It may seem that there remains a gap to be filled. Our explanation turns on considering a sentence like

(49)   "I believe that p but I do not know that I believe it"

as a special case of (9). There may seem, however, to be an important difference here. The absurdity of (9) has in general no tendency at all to reflect on the corresponding sentences in the third person, say on

(50)   "p but a does not know that p"

(where a is a name or a third-person pronoun), while in our explanation we assumed that the absurdity of (49) tends to be transferred to such third-person sentences as

(49)(a)   "a believes that p but he does not know that he believes it."

Why this difference?

The difference, it seems to me, is mainly a factual one. However self-defeating it may be to say "It is raining but I don't know that it is" it is perfectly natural to say "It is raining but he does not know that it is": we can easily imagine circumstances in which the latter might be an appropriate thing to say. When it comes to one's beliefs, however, it is much harder to imagine circumstances in which I can know something about the beliefs of another man that he does not know himself.[14] Normally one

---

[14] It is sometimes possible to come to know that somebody fails to know (or to believe) something although he *does not* himself know his failure by ascertaining that he *cannot* be said to know anything at all. Thus sentences like "He is asleep and doesn't know you've come home" or "He is an idiot and doesn't know anything" are completely in order. However, this is beside our present purpose; we are here interested

knows far better than anybody else what one knows and what one believes. When this *de facto* unlikelihood complements the logical absurdity of (49), philosophers are led to overlook the fact that (49)(a) need not always have anything strange about it.

This serves to explain why the force of epistemic implications is felt especially strongly in the case of sentences containing such quasi-psychological verbs as "believes," "knows," and the like. (Their force is of course felt still more strongly when we have to do with verbs which can really be said to express "states of mind.") The more difficult it is for others to know whether such sentences are true or not, the more temptation there is to extend the absurdity of epistemically indefensible sentences to the corresponding sentences in the third person. If it were always impossible for others really to know what their fellow men believe, then sentences of the form (49)(a) would not have any use in the third (or in the second) person. Since the corresponding first-person sentences are epistemically indefensible and in that sense absurd, it would then be literally true that all sentences of the form (49)(a) are always absurd: we could never deny that one knows what one believes. In this sense, it may be said that if it were impossible for *others* to know what one believes or knows, one would necessarily have to know it *oneself*. In a sense, the myth of the self-illumination of certain mental activities is therefore a consequence of the myth of one's privileged access to them.

4.16.   *Thinking that one may be mistaken.* If *a* is the first-person singular pronoun "I," there is a very natural way of reading the sentence

---

primarily in the question what people who are in full command of their faculties may be said to know or not to know. In the sense of knowing in which a sleeping man does not know what he believes, he cannot be said to know anything at all.

(51)   "$B_a p$ & $P_a \sim p$"

namely, "I believe that p but I may be mistaken," meaning, of course, that it is possible, for all I know, that I should be mistaken. The reader is invited to verify that (51) is epistemically and doxastically defensible. The defensibility of "$K_a(B_a p$ & $P_a \sim p)$" may be said to show that I can think it possible that I am mistaken in believing that p; I can even know that it is possible. This may go some way toward solving A. M. MacIver's interesting problem as to how it is possible to think this.[15] One of the sources of confusion here is the difficulty of expressing the difference between (51) and such expressions as

(51)(a)   "$B_a p$ & $C_a \sim p$,"

(51)(b)   "p & $C_a \sim p$,"

and

(51)(c)   "p & $P_a \sim p$"

in ordinary language; we are tempted to read all of them pretty much in the same way. There is, however, a distinction with vengeance here: although (51) is defensible both epistemically and doxastically, (51)(c) is indefensible epistemically; (51)(b) is indefensible epistemically and doxastically; while (51)(a) even indefensible *simpliciter*.

4.17. *An analogue to Moore's paradox for the second person*. It was already pointed out that in a sense the absurdity of (8) does not turn on the peculiarities of the first-person singular pronoun, namely, in the sense that (30)* is indefensible no matter what a is. Similarly, (40)* and (41) are indefensible no matter what a is. In this sense, the absurdity of (9) does not depend on the special uses the verb *know* may have in the first person singular.

---

[15] See *Analysis*, XVII (1956), 25–30.

This fact may also be brought out by observing that the indefensibility of (41) is reflected by sentences which are not in the first person but in the second. Uttering the sentence

(52)   "*p* but you do not know that *p*"

may sometimes be distinctly odd, unless the speaker is taken to mean

"*p* but you did not know that *p*."

The occasional oddity of (52) is not very difficult to account for. The first and foremost purpose of addressing a statement to somebody is to inform him of something. Addressing a statement to the person referred to by *a* is in fact often called "letting *a* know something." Now uttering a sentence can only serve this purpose if it is possible for the person to whom it is addressed to know the truth of what he is being told. Thus if (52) is to serve the normal purpose of declarative second-person sentences, it must be possible for you to know what you are being told, that is, the sentence

(53)   "You know that the case is as follows: *p* but you do not know that *p*"

must be defensible. But (53) is of the form (41) and therefore indefensible. In other words, (52) is an abnormal sentence in that it cannot ever be used to let the person to whom it is addressed know what this sentence expresses, for he cannot conceivably know it. For this reason, I submit, (52) is sometimes felt to be somewhat odd.

Of course, what (52) expresses may very well be true. It may even be known to be true. But it can remain true only as long as it remains *sotto voce*. If you know that I am well informed and if I address the words (52) to you, these words have a curious effect which may perhaps be called antiperformatory.[16] You may come to know that what I say *was* true, but saying it in so many words has the effect of making what is being said false. In a way, this is exactly opposite to what happens with some typical utterances called performatory. In appropriate circumstances, uttering the words "I promise" is to make a promise, that is, to bring about a state of affairs in which it is true to say that I promised. In contrast, uttering (52) in circumstances where the speaker is known to be well informed has the opposite effect of making what is being said false.

Of course, the antiperformatory effect may be just what the speaker wants to accomplish. Whenever this is understood, statements of the form (52) become intelligible.[17] They are then merely somewhat roundabout ways of letting you know that *p*. For instance, the sentence

"You don't know it but your essay has won the prize"
would naturally be understood in this way, that is, as a way of telling you that, however surprising it may be to you, your essay *has* won the prize.

---

[16] Please do not misunderstand this term. As it is used here, it merely serves to contrast the *effects* which uttering (52) may have with the *effects* of some of the best-known utterances which Austin and others have called performatory (performative). A *statement* of the form (52) is of course performatory in the broad sense in which we have been using the term: its peculiarities are due to a performance (an utterance) rather than to the uttered sentence as such. The effects of (52) are in fact a special case of the performatory effects of epistemically (or doxastically) indefensible statements.

[17] I do not claim that this is the only way of making sense of (52). There may be other circumstances, albeit unusual ones, in which (52) may be intelligible. Witness, e.g., a psychiatrist saying to patient "You don't know it but you really hate your father." Here an instance of (52) amounts to an allegation of self-deception.

4.18. *A generalization.* The peculiarity of (8) was generalized by means of the notion of doxastic indefensibility and the peculiarity of (9) by means of the notion of epistemic indefensibility. Similarly, the peculiarity of (52) may be generalized by a related notion. The new notion is in fact closely related to the old ones. We shall say that whenever a set of statements is epistemically indefensible for the person referred to by *b* to make, then it will also be epistemically indefensible for anybody to address these statements to him. The most important case in which this new notion differs from the old ones is that in which the statements contain pronouns in the second person singular. Such pronouns cannot but refer to the person to whom the statements are addressed. Of sets of sentences containing such pronouns we can say that they are or are not epistemically indefensible without specifying to whom they are assumed to be addressed.

There is an interesting difference between epistemically indefensible sentences in the second person and epistemically (or doxastically) indefensible sentences in the first person. In both cases, their peculiarity is of performatory character. In the case of second-person sentences, this performance has to be that of actually uttering the sentence in question or, more explicitly, that of addressing it to somebody. On the other hand, in the case of first-person sentences we cannot limit to overt utterances the performances through which the doxastically (or, to smaller extent, epistemically) indefensible sentences defeat themselves. (Cf. section 4.10.) The reason is fairly obvious. In order to become aware of what I have on my mind I do not have to utter any words in the way I normally have to utter them in order to make you aware of it. For instance, in the case of a doxastically indefensible sentence the performance through which its absurdity manifests itself may be merely an act of thinking, more specifically, an act of trying to believe what the sentence expresses. What we have arrived at is therefore a partial analogy between overt speech-acts and more or less private thought-acts. It would be suggestive to try to generalize this analogy and to view the notion of thinking as an "analogical extension" of the notion of saying. An interesting attempt in this direction has in fact been made by Peter Geach.[18] Thinking, on this view, is not so much an interior monologue as an interior dialogue; a view anticipated in Plato's dictum that "in thinking the soul is conversing with herself." Closely similar views were also expressed by C. S. Peirce.[19]

4.19.   *The privileges of the first person.*   The fact that paradoxical (epistemically indefensible) statements can be made in the second person and not just in the first also serves to call our attention to an interesting feature they have in common. The sentence

(9)   "p but I do not know whether p"

and therefore also the sentence

"p but I do not know that p"

was seen to be absurd (in the sense of being epistemically indefensible for anybody to make), and the sentence

(52)   "p but you do not know that p"

was also seen to be self-defeating (in the sense of being epistemically indefensible to be addressed to anybody). Why, then, are the corresponding sentences in the third person, for example,

(54)   "p but a does not know that p"

not self-defeating? The obvious answer may be put as follows: Uttering (54) may indeed be self-defeating pretty much in the

---

[18] *Mental Acts* (London, 1957), pp. 75 ff.

[19] See his *Collected Papers* (Cambridge, Mass., 1931–1958), VI, sec. 338, and V, sec. 421; cf. IV, sec. 6.

same way as uttering (9) or (52), namely, in case *a* happens to overhear what is being said. But such a case is merely accidental. It is not part and parcel of the logic of statements in the third person that the person referred to in them (by a third-person pronoun or by a name) should hear (or, rather, overhear) what is being said. In contrast, it is in a sense logically necessary that statements in the second person should be heard (or read) and understood by the person to whom they are addressed. Of course, he may fail to hear or to understand, but that amounts to a failure of communication. You either hear what is said to you or else you do not; you do not overhear it.

Paradoxical statements in the first person may be looked upon in the same light. If it is logically absurd for statements in the second person not to be heard and understood by the person to whom they are addressed, it is even more absurd for statements in the first person not to be heard and understood by the speaker (apart from Freudian and non-Freudian slips). As Wittgenstein points out, my relation to my words is different from other people's relation to them. I do not have to listen to my voice in order to know what I am saying. There is not a physical but a (so to speak) logical necessity of hearing what one is saying—if there were not, uttering (8) or (9) would not be any stranger than uttering (54).

This peculiarity of first-person statements may not be entirely unrelated to the idea that one's mind is transparent to oneself. We have seen that there is a sense in which one cannot help hearing—rather, knowing without listening—what one is saying. If we are also right in construing thinking as a sort of interior dialogue, then it is tempting to conclude that one must always be able to know what one is thinking, including what one knows and what one believes. If you are conversing with me, we cannot carry on a rational argument unless you hear and understand what I am saying. Is not the same true, it may be asked, when a "soul is conversing with herself"? The obvious, and correct, answer is "yes"; but the very comparison with second-person statements suggests that the logical parentage of this conceptual fact is different from what might be expected. If the notion of thinking is an analogical extension of the notion of saying, then the fact that one cannot fail to know what one is thinking is an analogical extension of the fact that one cannot fail to know what one is saying. We have also seen that this line of thought shows only that one always knows what one is thinking in the sense that not knowing it would be epistemically indefensible.

How close we have come to the actual doctrine of mind's automatic self-knowledge is shown by the fact that we have ended up endorsing, with heavy qualifications, one of the meta-phors by means of which the doctrine is often illustrated. When Gilbert Ryle explains the doctrine as follows, "To use another simile, mental processes are 'overheard' by the mind whose processes they are, somewhat as a speaker overhears the words he is himself uttering," [20] he is in fact giving us more than a simile. He is referring to one of the simple logical facts of which, it seems to me, the whole doctrine is an extension and a dramati-zation.

4.20. *Comparing different solutions to Moore's problem.* The ex-planation I offered for the absurdity of (8) may be compared with the older accounts of Moore's problem. I shall not discuss the earlier explanations systematically; I shall use them only to bring, by way of contrast, into a sharper focus certain features of my own explanation.

Moore bases his explanation of the oddity of (8) on the fact that in the great majority of cases we believe what we say. For this reason, anybody who says p thereby creates an expectation

---

[20] Gilbert Ryle, *The Concept of Mind* (London, 1949), p. 159.

that he believes that p is true. Moore expresses this by saying that one implies it by asserting the sentence in question, although it is not logically implied by one's words. Hence the second part of (8) contradicts something which is implied by uttering the first part. In short, the absurdity of (8) reflects the fact that "lying, though common enough, is vastly exceptional."

One soon begins to feel, however, that the absurdity of (8) cuts deeper than that of deliberate lying.[21] We are now in a position to see why this is so. If I am right, whoever utters (8) says something it is impossible for him to believe in the long run —which is here no longer than the simple deduction (33)–(39). And this impossibility is a consequence of the logical properties of (8). But lying (if it may be so called) in such a way that one's insincerity is betrayed by the very form of words one is using is not only vastly more exceptional than lying ever is; it is completely pointless.

Another shortcoming of Moore's account is that it does not help us to understand the queerness of the related form of words (9). For it is quite usual for people to say things they do not really know. Hence saying p does not imply (in Moore's sense) that the speaker knows that p is true; hence the two parts of (9) do not contradict each other even by implication (in Moore's sense). Nevertheless, statements of the form (9) are sometimes distinctly odd in a way which requires an explanation.

Max Black has criticized Moore's account of (8) and offered one of his own. Very briefly, the gist of his remarks may perhaps be expressed as follows: It is a presupposition of the notion of honest assertion that the speaker believes what he says. Now the notion of assertion has to be understood, according to Black, in terms of the notion of honest assertion, not vice versa. Hence

---

[21] This point is made very well by Max Black in "Saying and Disbelieving," *op. cit.*

(and here I am perhaps filling in Black's argument a little) we cannot have a genuine assertion when it is obvious that the pre-suppositions of honest assertion are not fulfilled. A sentence of the form (8) is a case in point.

In more detail, the presuppositions of honest assertion fail to be satisfied by (8) (according to Black) for the following reason: When one utters p in the conventional (assertive) tone of voice, one thereby signifies that one believes what one says. This signification of the first part of (8) conflicts with what is said in the second part of (8). Hence its absurdity.

I shall not criticize here Black's account as far as it goes; I shall merely argue that it requires complementation (and modifica-tion) in order to do the same job as the alternative account offered in this essay. For one thing, Black's account does not help us to understand why (9) is logically odd. (It was, of course, not designed by Black to do this; for this reason, my remarks should not be construed as criticism.) It cannot very well be a presupposition of the notion of honest assertion that the speaker knows what he says; one may be honestly mistaken. Hence (9) does not violate the presuppositions of honest assertion in the way (8) does.

Here one may perhaps attempt to replace the notion of honest assertion by that of honest *and true* assertion. One can, it seems to me, really make a case to the effect that this notion is more primary logically than that of assertion. (Think of the ways in which the notion of assertion can be learned.) In this way, Black's account may perhaps be modified so as to account for the absurdity of (9), too.

But notice that even then the details of Black's account of how the absurdity comes about have to be modified in order to be applicable to (9). There may be a special tone of voice which signifies belief, but highly doubtful whether there is a corresponding "tone of knowledge." At any rate, the contrary has been claimed by Wittgenstein.[22] Hence I doubt that there can be a conflict between what is signified by the first part of (9) and what is said in the second part comparable with the conflict Black finds in (8).

4.21. *The economy of our solution.* It seems to be a virtue of my explanation of the absurdity of (8) that it is more economical than the earlier accounts of the same absurdity. I do not have to assume that, whenever one makes a statement (say, utters q) under normal conditions and in a normal tone of voice, there is a presumption that one believes that q is true. It suffices for my purposes to assume that, whenever one utters q, there is a presumption that one conceivably can believe what one says (in the sense that q must not be obviously indefensible). At the very least, it may be assumed that one is not depriving oneself of this possibility by the very form of words one is using. This assumption is weaker[23] than the assumptions that are implicit in Black's account of the absurdity of (8).

Even this assumption is not indispensable. I do not think that only such forms of words make sense as can be uttered and believed (or known) by the utterer. The fact rather seems to be that forms of words which do not meet this requirement are useless for most of the purposes which our language is expected to serve. It is obvious that honest communication of information cannot take place by means of statements which cannot be believed (or which cannot be known) by their makers. More inter-

---

[22] See Malcolm, *Ludwig Wittgenstein: A Memoir*, p. 92.

[23] It is by weakening our assumptions in this way that we are able to extend our explanation from (8) to (9). It is not absurd to say something one does not know; but it is often absurd to say something one cannot possibly know, particularly if the impossibility is shown by the form of words one is using.

estingly, it was already pointed out that lying is impossible by means of sentences like (8) which automatically betray the speaker's lack of conviction.

We might say that uttering Moore's sentence is paradoxical because certain presuppositions of ours are not fulfilled. But these presuppositions are not merely presuppositions which must be fulfilled in order that we would speak of an honest assertion, as Black suggests. They are presuppositions which must be fulfilled in order that the utterance is to serve any normal or even some slightly abnormal purpose which utterances may be calculated to serve. We are not here dealing with the presuppositions of the use of some particular word or phrase but with the presuppositions of the successful use of any declarative sentence.

There may be special contexts, however, in which even an obvious failure on the part of the speaker to believe or to know what he is saying does not defeat his purpose or at least is not as destructive to his purposes as in other, more common circumstances. The existence of contexts of this kind—as well as the existence of variants of (8) and of (9) which are less absurd than the originals—is relevant to our inquiry in more than one way. So far, I have not indicated whether all the instances of (8) and (9) are equally absurd, or whether their absurdity can be removed by relatively small modifications. Now it is time to be more specific in this respect. At the same time, the existence of contexts where (8) and (9) are less absurd than in others gives us an opportunity of putting our theory to a test. If my analysis of the reasons for the absurdity of (8) and (9) is right, we may expect that it can be adapted to explain these exceptions as well.

My explanation of the absurdity of (9) was based on the fact that it is impossible for the utterer of (9) to know the truth of what he is saying, in the sense that (40) is indefensible. If this is the case, we may expect that (9) is less absurd in contexts where the failure to know what one is saying does not matter or is not particularly important. A case in point seems to be the statement

(55) "God is almighty although I don't know that He is."

The relative naturalness of (55) may be seen by comparing it with such a (putative) statement as

(56) "Phosphorus melts at 44°C. but I do not know that it does."

If I am right, the former is more natural than the latter because the purposes of religious discourse are not normally defeated by the speaker's failure to know what he is saying in the way the purposes of scientific (factual) discourse are thereby defeated.

This suggests that the absurdity of (9) is not due simply and solely to the impossibility of knowing the truth of what (9) expresses. Its absurdity is partly due to the absence of any indication of some special circumstances which would relieve one from the normal expectation that one can know what one is saying, as well as to the absence of any disclaimer which would indicate that the speaker is alive to the fact and ready to admit that he cannot know what he is saying. One way of giving a hint to this effect is to give in (9) the word "know" an emphatic stress:

(57) "*p* but I don't *know* that *p*"

is perceptibly less awkward than (9). (One may say, e.g., "The Republicans will win in 1964; well, I don't *know* that they will win.") That it is, is not difficult to explain. One possible (partial) explanation is as follows: Emphasizing the verb "know" is calculated to call attention to the other verbs which could enter into the same construction (or into the corresponding positive construction) instead of "know." The most prominent verb of this kind is "believe." Hence the stressing of "know" in (9) has the effect of assimilating (57) to (47). And (47), as we saw, is in all respects a perfectly natural statement.

Much the same remarks pertain to (8). Its absurdity is not simply due to the obviousness of the impossibility of believing what one is saying when uttering (8). There may be situations in which I do not believe what I am saying, and yet do not care at all whether or not this fact is obvious to others. For instance, I may find a piece of news so unexpected that it is natural for me to say that I cannot believe it. The absurdity of (8) is partly due to the absence of any indication of some special circumstances which would relieve the speaker from the normal expectation that he can conceivably believe what he is saying. It is interesting to observe that one way of giving such an indication is to strengthen (logically speaking) (8) to

(58)   "p but I cannot believe that p."

If p expresses a somewhat unexpected fact, (58) may be a fairly natural form of words. One may find oneself saying, quite spontaneously,

(59)   "September is here already. I cannot believe it."

That (58) is more natural than (8) may perhaps be explained as follows: If I say: "I cannot believe that p," I imply that I am aware that I should believe that p is true but that I fail to do so. Since p is part of (8)—and of (58)—this also amounts to an admission of a failure to believe the whole of (8) or of (58).[24] Such an admission shows that the speaker is aware that his statement cannot serve most of the normal purposes our state-

----

[24] I do not think that this is the only way of making sense of statements of the form (58). Another way might be to assume that the speaker is violating the assumption (b) of section 1.3, i.e., that he is caught in the act of changing his mind. In this way, we may perhaps understand such a statement as the following: "It is thundering—but I cannot believe it, for there are no clouds anywhere." Here this interpretation is suggested by the fact that the speaker goes on to give a reason for his change of mind.

ments usually serve. It constitutes an invitation to interpret the statement in some unusual way, for example, as a "mere" expression of surprise.

Be this as it may, comparison between (8) and (58) is instructive in several respects. It shows graphically that the absurdity of (8) is not that of a logical contradiction or of what we have called indefensibility. For obviously (8) is implied by (58). Hence any contradiction entailed by (8) will likewise be entailed by (58). Yet (58) is clearly less absurd than (8).

It may also be pointed out that Black's account of the absurdity of (8) does not help us to understand the relation of (8) and (58). On the contrary, it leads us to expect that (58) is at least as absurd as (8). For whatever is signified by uttering p in a particular tone of voice is as likely to conflict with "I cannot believe that p" as with "I do not believe that p." If I am right, this expectation is not fulfilled.

Five

Knowing that One Knows

5.1. *The meaning of "knowing that one knows" is not clear.* By means of the methods we developed in Chapters Two and Three we may also study forms of words whose uses in ordinary discourse are not clearly defined. Concerning such sentences it would be rash to maintain that they have (in ordinary language) a definite meaning which we are only elucidating by means of our rules and conditions. Nevertheless, our methods enable us to approach even forms of words whose meaning depends on the circumstances in which they are uttered. In a sense, we can *give* them a definite meaning. We may assume, for a moment, that our conditions are correct, and see what these problematic statements will turn out to mean on this assumption. If we are on the right track, we should then be able to explain why these particular types of (putative) statements are less clear-cut than others, why their meaning easily fluctuates, and how the different possible senses come about. In this way, a study of the pathological cases may serve to confirm our analysis, and thereby throw back light on perfectly ordinary cases.

In this vein, it may be asked why, for example, the form of words

(60)   "I know that I know that p"

is rather strange while a closely related statement like

(61)   "He knows that I know that p"

is perfectly natural. The problematic character of (60) may be seen, for example, by asking how one would go about verifying or falsifying (60), or what my state of mind would be like if (60) were true or false. It is obviously far from clear what is meant by (60).

5.2.   *"Knowing that one knows" virtually equivalent to "knowing."* I shall begin discussing (60) by asking what is the relation of (60) to the simpler sentence

(62)   "I know that p."

Here (60) and (62) are of the form

(63)   "K_aK_ap"

and

(64)   "K_ap"

respectively. We are therefore called upon to inquire into the relation between (63) and (64) in general.

My answer to the main question is very simple: (63) and (64)—and a fortiori (60) and (62)—are *virtually equivalent*.

This may be shown by proving that (63) and (64) virtually imply each other. These two proofs follow the familiar reductive strategy. As usual, my arguments may be thought of as abortive attempts to describe consistently certain states of affairs, in the present case states of affairs in which either both "K_aK_ap" and "$\sim K_ap$" or both "K_ap" and "$\sim K_aK_ap$" are true.

The first attempt fails trivially, for sentences of the form "$K_a q$" and "$\sim q$" cannot enter into one and the same model set in virtue of (C.K) and (C.$\sim$). The second attempt may proceed as follows:

(65) "$K_a p$" ϵ μ ⎫
(66) "$\sim K_a K_a p$" ϵ μ ⎬ by assumption;

(67) "$P_a \sim K_a p$" ϵ μ from (66) by (C.$\sim$K);

(68) "$\sim K_a p$" ϵ μ^* from (67) by (C.P*) (μ^* is an alternative to μ with respect to a);

(69) "$K_a p$" ϵ μ^* from (65) by (C.KK*).

The outcome of the attempted construction is thus a violation of (C.$\sim$). This violation completes our reductive proof, showing that "$K_a p$" virtually implies "$K_a K_a p$."

Since this proof is a rather short one, it may be expected that the force of the virtual implication which is demonstrated thereby is felt, however inarticulately, by those who actually employ the notions of knowledge and belief.[1]

---

[1] In his contribution to the symposium "Is There Only One Correct System of Modal Logic?" (*Proceedings of the Aristotelian Society*, Sup. Vol. XXXIII [1959], 23–40), E. J. Lemmon rejects (p. 39) the implication from (64) to (63). He rejects it in spite of the fact that he is not concerned with active knowledge but only with "a kind of logical fiction, the rational man" who (implicitly) knows all the consequences of what he knows. Hence Lemmon seems to be concerned, in effect, with the same notions as we; he seems to reject the virtual implication from (64) to (63). This would be rather serious for our purposes, for rejecting this virtual implication would necessitate rejecting the condition (C.KK*) on which the proof of the implication rests. Lemmon's reasons are not, however, valid against what I have said. They are in terms of what "the rational man" might (rationally?) forget. They are therefore

Our proof therefore shows that, in a sense, you cannot know anything without knowing that you know it. Notice, however, that you may fail—unless you happen to be as sagacious as Socrates—to know your ignorance. For "$\sim K_a p$" does not imply (virtually imply) "$K_a \sim K_a p$," as you may easily verify.[2]

The use of the condition (C.KK*) in the argument (65)–(69) occasions a qualification to its outcome similar to others we have encountered earlier. The (virtual) implication from (64) to (63) obtains only if the person referred to by a knows that he is referred to by it, for this was seen to be a prerequisite of the applicability of (C.KK*). It may be worth while to observe that the corresponding implication *in the first person* (from "I know that p" to "I know that I know that p") is none the worse for this qualification.

5.3. *On the history of the problem of "knowing that one knows."* I have shown that (60) and (62)—more generally, (63) and (64) —are virtually equivalent. In a sense, they have exactly the same logical powers. But are we right in expecting that the force of

---

ruled out by the initial provision that only statements made on one and the same occasion are considered here. See sec. 1.3, condition (a).

Incidentally, I do not think that Lemmon's choice of the term "rational" is particularly happy, in spite of the fact that I have myself made use of the same term earlier in the present essay and in spite of the fact that it is related to some of the uses of "rational" (in the sense of "reasonable") in the law. Making statements of the kind I have called indefensible need not always be irrational. What is irrational indeed is the behavior of a man who would persist in subscribing to an indefensible statement after its indefensibility has been made known to him.

[2] The fact that the former implies the latter epistemically need not destroy the difference between you and Socrates. There sometimes is an element of self-deception in a failure to recognize an epistemic implication. Socrates recognized his ignorance, it may be said, because he knew himself.

this equivalence is somehow felt by those who actually employ such locutions as (60)?

It was already observed that we are not likely to get definite answers from the speakers of "ordinary language." Such logically quaint expressions have nevertheless always fascinated philosophers, who have not hesitated to commit themselves on their meaning. The relation of (60) to (62) has been frequently discussed by philosophers, ancient as well as recent. It is not my purpose to recount the history of the problem of self-knowledge here. It is, however, worth while to recall some representative opinions so as to see in what direction the views of philosophers tend and what kinds of reasons they have offered for their views.

The consensus of philosophers seems to support overwhelmingly the equivalence of (63) and (64) just as we were led to expect. The problem of "knowledge about knowledge" was discussed at length by Plato in the *Charmides*. The discussion seems to indicate that Plato thought it impossible to disentangle "knowledge about knowledge" from knowledge *simpliciter*, except perhaps in some secondary and unimportant sense of knowing.[3] More explicitly, Aristotle went on record as identifying knowing and knowing that one knows.[4] St. Augustine, too, made important use of the equivalence.[5] Aristotle was followed by some of the most influential mediaeval authors, among others Averroës[6] and St. Thomas Aquinas.[7] On this point Spinoza was

----

[3] See *Charmides* 169 E ff.

[4] See *Nicomachean Ethics* IX, 9, 1170^{a}27 ff., *Eudemian Ethics* VII, 12, 1245^{a}6 ff.; cf. also *De Anima* III, 4, 429^{b}26–430^{a}9, *Metaphysics* XII, 7, 1072^{b}20 and 9, 1074^{b}33 ff.

[5] In *De Trinitate* XV, xii, 21; cf. also X, xi, 18.

[6] See *Tahafut al-Tahafut*, tr. with introduction and notes by S. van den Bergh (London, 1954), pp. 209–212.

[7] *Summa Theologica* II, 1, quest. 112, art. 5, obj. 2, and reply thereto; cf. *Questiones de Quolibet* III, art. 9, ad resp. I am indebted to Peter Geach for these references.

a faithful Aristotelian, as witnessed both by the *Ethics*[8] and by his treatise *On the Improvement of the Understanding*.[9] The implication from knowing to knowing that one knows is implicit in Locke's account of personal identity [10] and explicit in Samuel Clarke's *Second Defense of an Argument*.[11] More recently the implication has been recognized by philosophers as different as idealists of various persuasions (e.g., Schopenhauer and Sir William Hamilton) and the Oxford realists Cook Wilson and Prichard.[12] And quite recently the equivalence of (60) with (62) was suggested by Richard Taylor as a solution to a certain puzzle of his.[13]

Perhaps the simplest argument for the equivalence comes from Schopenhauer, according to whom "your knowing that you know only differs in words from your knowing" and " 'I know that I know' means nothing more than 'I know.' . . ." In fact, Schopenhauer's reasons are not unrelated to ours: "If your knowing and your knowing that you know are two different things, just try to separate them, and first to know without knowing that you know, then to know that you know, without this knowledge being at the same time knowing." [14] What I did in the argument (65)–(69) can be interpreted as an attempt to

---

[8] *Ethics* II, propositions 21 and 43; *The Chief Works of Benedict de Spinoza*, tr. by R. H. M. Elwes (London, 1905–1906), II, 102–103, 114–115.

[9] *The Chief Works of Benedict de Spinoza*, II, 12–14.

[10] *An Essay concerning Human Understanding*, bk. II, ch. xxvii, sec. 11.

[11] London, 1707; quoted by C. S. Lewis in *Studies in Words* (Cambridge, Eng., 1960), p. 211.

[12] For John Cook Wilson, see his *Statement and Inference* (London, 1926), I, 107; for H. A. Prichard, see *Knowledge and Perception* (London, 1950), pp. 86, 88, 96, and *passim*.

[13] *Analysis*, XVI (1955), 63–65.

[14] *Ueber die vierfache Wurzel des Satzes vom zureichenden Grunde*, ch. vii, sec. 41. The translation is from Arthur Schopenhauer, *Two Essays*, tr. by Mme Karl Hillebrand (London, 1891), p. 166.

do just what the old pessimist suggests: We tried to see what a state of affairs would be like in which one would know without thereby knowing that one knows, or knows that one knows without knowing *simpliciter*, and we found that such states of affairs cannot be consistently described.

Schopenhauer's argument does not depend on any psychological or quasi-psychological theory. It is, I am tempted to say, an almost direct appeal to our logical common sense.

The equivalence of (60) and (62) has been defended, however, in more sophisticated terms. The views of the late Professor Prichard are a well-known case in point.[15] He formulates the equivalence by saying that "we must recognize that whenever we know something we either do, or at least can, by reflecting, directly know that we are knowing it." This may seem to be very close to what we have been saying. But it is important to realize that Prichard's qualification ("can, by reflecting") is entirely different from the qualifications we made in Chapter Two. By "reflecting," Prichard does not mean "reflecting on the consequences of what we know" but "reflecting on our state of mind" or, as he puts it, by reflecting on "our condition" (p. 88). His arguments for the (virtual) equivalence of (60) and (62) are therefore in effect arguments from introspection (cf. sections 3.8–3.9). He is defending a correct principle by means of arguments we cannot accept.

This is also shown by the fact that Prichard's arguments prove too much, as arguments from introspection easily do. For he goes on to say (p. 86): ". . . and that whenever we believe something, we similarly either do or can know that we are believing it and not knowing it." If I am right, the proper doxastic analogue to "$K_a p \supset K_a K_a p$" is "$B_a p \supset B_a B_a p$" which may be seen to be

---

[15] *Knowledge and Perception*, pp. 86, 88, 96, etc. A different reconstruction of Prichard's point has been given by Malcolm in "Knowledge and Belief," *op. cit.*, pp. 178–189.

self-sustaining by an argument which parallels (65)–(69), whereas it is easily seen that "$B_a p \supset K_a B_a p$" is not self-sustaining unless (C.BB*ep) or (C.BK) is adopted. And in sections 3.7–3.8 we found reasons for rejecting them. Nor is the implication "$(B_a p \,\&\, \sim K_a p) \supset K_a(B_a p \,\&\, \sim K_a p)$," which may be a more faithful representation of Prichard's intentions, self-sustaining. Hence Prichard does not seem to be entirely right here.[16] Of course, all the implications in question become correct when *a* is taken to be the first-person singular pronoun "I" and when they are reconstrued as *epistemic* implications. This fact may have been operative in Prichard's case. If so, his mistake is merely the very common one of not distinguishing the different implications from each other.

5.4.   *The basis of the equivalence.*   I have not discussed the history of our problem to extol Schopenhauer or to criticize Prichard. I have done it in order to make clear that our reasons for adopting the virtual equivalence of (63) and (64) are different from the traditional ones. The equivalence was proved by means of (C.KK*). Earlier, it was pointed out that the applications of this condition in reductive proofs can be replaced by applications of the rule (A.PKK*). In fact, the steps (68) and (69) of our argument may be compressed into one application of (A.PKK*). Thus it is (C.KK*) or, if you prefer, (A.PKK*) that the equivalence really turns on. It is not based on psycho-

---

[16] This need not defeat all the uses Prichard makes of his first thesis, however. Among other things, there is (if I am right) a solid logical fact underlying his insistence that questions of the form "Do I know that I know that *p*?" do not constitute a subject matter independent of the questions "Do I know that *p*?" See H. A. Prichard, "Does Moral Philosophy Rest on a Mistake?" *Mind*, N.S. XXI (1912), 21–37; reprinted in *Readings in Ethical Theory*, ed. by W. Sellars and John Hospers (New York, 1952), pp. 149–162, especially pp. 160–161; and in Prichard's *Moral Obligation* (Oxford, 1949), pp. 1–17.

logical or quasi-psychological evidence. If you want to see in the equivalence a reflection of a more interesting truth, you may try the quasi-performatory character of "I know"-statements (cf. section 3.8) rather than the transparency of our minds. I do not think, however, that (A.PKK*) is really in need of any more evidence than we gave in section 2.2.

Hence the arguments we gave for the equivalence of (63) and (64) are entirely different from the traditional introspective arguments. Ours are logical rather than quasi-psychological. This is interesting in view of the criticisms to which arguments from introspection have been subjected. Gilbert Ryle and others have criticized the view that such "states of mind" as knowledge and belief are "self-intimating" by criticizing the idea of a mind's immediate awareness of its own states. We have in this chapter restored one of the conclusions Ryle rejected, namely, that knowing something virtually implies knowing that one knows. We have done this by means of arguments which are immune to Ryle's criticism. Just because we have given up the idea that knowledge is a state of mind we can now say that knowing that one knows "only differs in words from knowing." [17] For now the virtual implication from (64) to (63) need not mean that one is performing, whenever one knows something, another act of self-observation. It will simply mean that all those circumstances which would justify one in saying "I know" will also justify one in saying "I know that I know." Since the implication depends essentially on (C.KK*)—or (A.PKK*), if you want—it may also be said that just because an "I know that"-statement is *in general* open to criticisms which admit that what you claim to know does hold but deny that you *knew* it, just for this reason such criticisms are necessarily empty in the *particular* case of "knowing that you know"; here the only relevant criticism

---

[17] Subject to the qualifications which we shall discuss in the remaining sections of this chapter.

is that you do not know. In any case, it is salutary to observe that one of the principles Ryle seems to have included within the scope of his criticism can be restored by giving the expression "knowing that one knows" a sense which makes it immune to his criticism—or, rather, by showing that this new sense of the expression is (logically speaking) the normal one in contradistinction to the other senses which it may perhaps be given.

5.5. *The limitations of a virtual equivalence.* At this point, it may likewise be salutary to have a closer look at our own conclusions. Schopenhauer and company notwithstanding, qualifications are indeed in order. What we have shown is that (63) and (64) are *virtually* equivalent. From this it does not follow that statements in which one of them is asserted and the other denied are nonsensical. On the contrary, statements of the form

(70) "*a* knows that *p* but he does not know that he knows"

may very well have uses in more or less ordinary discourse. If Sophocles had made the Chorus say about Oedipus (at a moment when the audience already is in a position to know the truth): "He knows that he is himself the murderer of Laius, but he does not know yet that he knows," we would understand what is meant by these words. This does not tell against our theory, however. On the contrary, the meaning these words bear here is predictable by means of our general theory, including the considerations presented in sections 2.6 to 2.9. These considerations show what the fact that (70) is indefensible amounts to here. This statement is not one which cannot reasonably be made, but it is one whose truth depends on the failure of the person referred to by *a* to follow the implications of what he knows far enough. Hence asserting (70) naturally suggests that *a* is not aware of all the consequences of what he (actively) knows, in particular that he has not perceived that *p* follows from what he (actively) knows. And this, it seems to me, is likely to be one of the ways (70) may be understood.

It is instructive to compare (70) with what we obtain from it by switching to the first person singular:

(71)   "I know that p but I do not know that I know."

This is absurd in a way (70) is not. A reason for this absurdity is implicit in what has been said. We were able to give (70) a sense by taking it to mean that a has not noticed that p follows from what he (actively) knows. But this does not work for statements in the first person. It might be true of some p or other that it follows from what I know although I have not noticed it; but I cannot myself specify a particular p of this kind without making my statement self-defeating. For this reason (among others), (71) is more absurd than (70). (For the other reasons, see section 5.9.)

5.6.   *Virtual equivalence does not preclude a difference in meaning.*   In general, we can explain why (60) and (63) are comparatively rare in ordinary discourse. Just because they are virtually equivalent to the simpler forms of words (62) and (64), respectively, there is ordinarily no point in using them. What can be expressed by their means can be expressed more readily by means of the shorter and simpler expressions. Hence they are not normally used.

Notice that I do not have to claim—and that I do not claim—that what is meant by uttering (60) or (63) on the rare occasions at which they are uttered is exactly the same as would be meant by uttering (62) or (64), respectively, under the same circumstances. (In a sense, the expressions (63) and (64) mean the same, but we have to distinguish what a form of words means from what is meant by uttering them.) Since the longer forms of words (60) and (63) mean the same as the shorter forms (62)

and (64)—in the sense of being virtually equivalent to them—
nobody is likely to use them unless he aims at some special effect
which he wants to accomplish by using the more cumbersome
expressions.

One possible effect of this kind was already commented on.
It may be said to consist in indicating that the person in question
is aware that he is in a position to know. Another effect might
be to indicate that he feels certain ("is certain") that he knows.
Philosophers often seem to assume that this sense is what "knowing that one knows" should be taken to mean. For instance, it is
being assumed by Spinoza when he writes: ". . . therefore he, who
has an adequate idea or knows a thing truly, must at the same
time have an adequate idea or true knowledge of his knowledge;
that is, obviously, he must be assured. Q.E.D." [18] Prichard, too,
seems to make this assumption; after having argued that whoever
knows something can, by reflecting, also know that he knows it,
he goes on to interpret this as meaning that whoever knows
something can always be certain that he knows and that the
doubts of a Descartes are therefore spurious. (Cf. also St. Thomas
Aquinas, *loc. cit.*)

This is not, however, the only possible sense of "knowing that
one knows" even when it means something different from knowing *simpliciter*. I suspect that it makes no sense to speak of *the*
sense of the former expression as distinguished from the meaning
of the latter. For it is typical of the "special effects" which
constitute this "residual meaning" that they may vary from
context to context. In any case, the different residual meanings
have to be kept apart. Confusing them has been a rich source of
fallacies in philosophy. For instance, it is a fallacy to try to use
the (virtual) equivalence of (63) and (64) to prove conclusions
about the virtual certainty there might be about our knowledge.

---

[18] *Chief Works*, II, 114.

Knowing that One Knows

Spinoza and Prichard may be right in holding that, in a sense, "I know" implies "I know that I know." They may also be right in holding that the latter phrase means, in a rather natural sense, that I feel certain that I know. They did not realize, however, that the two senses are not identical.

5.7. *A comparison with double negation.* The situation here is perhaps not altogether different from what we find in the more familiar instance of double negation. It is generally agreed that in correct modern English usage the result of a double negation is normally a positive sentence.[19] And it seems to me that, from the logical point of view, we are entitled to say that a doubly negated sentence means exactly the same as the original unnegated sentence. In any case, this is not contradicted by the fact that what is meant by uttering a doubly negated expression usually is something different from what would be meant by uttering the simple unnegated expression in the same context. For this is just what is to be expected. If the doubly negated expression has the same logical powers as the unnegated one, anybody who uses the former is likely to aim at some special effect which is not part of the basic logic of negation. Perhaps the most common effect of this kind is to signify hesitation or uncertainty on the part of the speaker.[20] But this is not the only possible effect. For instance, the double negative may signify diffidence; at other times, it may be ironical ("Having plenty of money is not without advantages") or calculated to suggest a qualification different from hesitation. Or the reason for using a double negative may simply be a stylistic[21] preference of involved construction.

---

[19] See Otto Jespersen, *Essentials of English Grammar* (London, 1933), 28.4₁.

[20] Jespersen, *loc. cit.*

[21] Stylistic, that is to say, in a rather old-fashioned sense of the word. A modern student of style is likely to be interested in the other "special

5.8. *The residual meanings of "knowing that one knows."* It must be recognized, of course, that there may often be good logical reasons why the extra meaning of double negation or, in our case, of "knowing that one knows" tends to be what it is. One possible residual meaning was already given an explanation in terms of the peculiarity of our notion of indefensibility. There may also be a logical reason why (63) could naturally be taken to mean

(63)₀ "*a* is certain that he knows that *p*."

This reason may be seen by considering (70), which is not an unnatural thing to be said about a man who has at his disposal all the information requisite for knowing that *p* but who is (say) too timid to make the claim. What (70) expresses under these circumstances is straightforward enough. If the view of Urmson mentioned in section 2.2 is right, (70) says in effect that the man in question would be right if he said, "I know that *p*," and that he would also be right if he said, "I don't know that I know." That this makes sense to say does not tell against the indefensibility of (70). For what the indefensibility amounts to here is simply that nobody can defensibly utter *both* the sentences "I know that *p*" and "I don't know that I know that *p*" on one and the same occasion. Whoever utters (70) is not likely to deny this. It seems to me that just because one cannot very well utter both these sentences (70) comes to indicate that the person referred to by *a* would *not* say "I know that *p*"; for if he said it, it would not be true any more than he could defensibly deny knowing that he knows that *p*. Hence (70) comes to mean something like "*a* is in a position to say, 'I know that *p*'; but he won't

---

effects" as well, and especially in a writer's choice between them; cf. Richard M. Ohmann, "Prolegomena to the Analysis of Prose Style," in *Style in Prose Fiction* ("English Institute Essays, 1958"), ed. by Harold C. Martin (New York, 1959).

say so," leaving it to the hearer to diagnose the reason of his failure to make the claim as timidity or as some other variant of uncertainty. And this, it seems to me, comes very close to one of the ways in which (70) could naturally be taken.[22]

A more systematic way of studying some of the residual meanings is as follows. A sentence of form (63) has a "residual meaning" in so far as it is not equivalent to (64). The proof we gave for the equivalence made use of (C.KK*) and of (C.∼K). It has already been pointed out that these conditions need not be satisfied by all the senses the verb *know* may occasionally have in ordinary speech. The residual meaning may therefore be due to the fact that the speaker is using the verb in a sense in which these conditions are not satisfied. It has already been pointed out that the condition (C.KK*) is not satisfied if by "knowing that p" we merely mean "being aware of the fact that p." [23] In a sense, it may also be said that this interpretation of the verb *know* fails to satisfy (C.∼K). We may, of course, try to save it by reinterpreting all the metalogical notions which pertain to the notion of awareness in the same way we interpreted the notions of inconsistency and validity as indefensibility and self-sustenance, respectively, in Chapter Two. But the new notions would turn out to be rather uninteresting, that is, not paralleled by interesting pragmatical notions. It is much less objectionable or strange to say "I am not aware that p" than to say "I do not know that p" when p follows from what I already know by a relatively simple argument. In this sense, it may be

---

[22] Or is the explanation perhaps much simpler? It may be suggested that a man who says "I know that I know" is likelier to feel sure of his knowledge than a man who simply says "I know" for the same reason as a man who says "It is a big big house" is likelier to have been impressed with its size than a man who merely says "It is a big house." I do not think that this is the whole story, however.

[23] See section 2.2 and remember that (C.KK*) and (A.PKK*) do the same job.

said that the notion of awareness is restricted to *active* awareness while the notion of knowledge is not restricted to *active* knowledge in quite the same way, and that the former notion therefore fails to satisfy $(C.\sim K)$.

A number of residual meanings may therefore be obtained by interpreting knowledge as awareness in (63). This reading may be applied to the first occurrence of the verb *know* (or, strictly speaking, of its symbolic representative 'K') in (63), to the second, or to both. Accordingly, (63) may be understood to mean one of the following things:

$(63)_1$ "*a* is aware that he knows that *p*."

$(63)_2$ "*a* knows that he is aware that *p*."

$(63)_3$ "*a* is aware that he is aware that *p*."

Here $(63)_1$ is the sense in which Oedipus did not know that he knew, although Sophocles had placed him into an appropriate evidential situation. That this is a natural meaning of $(63)_1$ could have been predicted by means of our proof of the implication from (64) to (63). For in this proof $(C.\sim K)$ was applied to the very occurrence of 'K' which in $(63)_1$ has been interpreted as merely indicating awareness; witness the step from (66) to (67). The reason why $(63)_1$ fails to be implied by (64) therefore lies in the failure of the assumption which underlies $(C.\sim K)$, that is, in the failure of the assumption that people attend to the consequences of what they know.[24]

---

[24] Hence the negation of $(63)_1$ naturally applies to a situation in which somebody is in a position to know something without being aware of it. The following is Lawrence Durrell's description of such a situation: " 'It is Amaril you're in love with' I said—rather, blurted out. . . . Suddenly a shutter seemed to roll back across my mind. I realised that this new fact which I was enunciating was one that I had always known, but without *being aware of the knowing*! Foolish as it was the distinction was a real one. Amaril was like a playing card which had always been

The third sentence $(63)_3$ gives what may be called the psychological sense of "knowing that one knows." When William James denied that knowing implies knowing that one knows, he clearly intended the phrase in this sense.[25] In so far as the philosophers he thereby criticized intended their words in the same sense, their views no doubt hailed from a confusion of this with the other senses of "knowing that one knows."

In contrast to $(63)_3$ the second sentence $(63)_2$ *is* virtually implied by "*a* knows that *p*," provided that the remaining occurrences of *know* are understood in the full sense of the word. For then it means that the person referred to by *a* has enough evidence to be justified in claiming that he *knows* that he is aware that *p* is the case, in contradistinction (say) to merely thinking he is. No more evidence is required for this than for the justification of the simpler claim (should he make it) that he knows that *p*. The reason why the implication obtains here is again implicit in the proof $(65)–(69)$. In this proof neither of the critical conditions $(C.\sim K)$ and $(C.KK^*)$ was applied to that particular occurrence of the verb *know* (or, rather, of 'K') in (63) which alone was changed in the transition from (63) to $(63)_2$. Hence the proof may be expected to carry through as it stands.[26]

Although $(63)_2$ thus is in a sense equivalent to (64), there may be a point in using the former rather than the latter if knowledge

---

there, lying before me on the table, face downwards. I had been aware of its existence but had never turned it over" (*Clea* [London, 1960], p. 256; the italics are Durrell's).

[25] *Op. cit.*, I, 274.

[26] Whether it carries through completely depends on whether (68) and (69) may be said to contradict each other when the interpretation of the second occurrence of *know* in (63)—and therefore the interpretation of the word in (68)—is changed. For our purposes, it suffices to observe that, as long as the change is not made explicit, (68) and (69) certainly contradict each other verbally.

is construed as awareness in the latter sentence, too. This is necessary, in fact, in order for the failure of (C.KK*) to make any difference to us; for the single application of this condition in the proof (65)–(69) was to the occurrence of the verb *know* in (64). On this interpretation, (70) will simply mean that the person referred to by *a* is aware that *p* but that he does not really know it, that is, his awareness is not based on information which would justify a claim to knowledge; for we have just seen that "knowing that one is aware" is tantamount to knowing in the full (primary) sense of the word. In other words, in so far as (63) is construed as (63)₂ the iteration of the words "knows that" merely serves to indicate that they are being used in their full sense. There is no doubt that (63) is occasionally used in this way; I once heard a doctor saying to an impatient patient who felt much more certain of the diagnosis than the doctor himself: "Maybe you know what is wrong with you; but do you know that you know?" [27]

Here, and in similar situations, one may be inclined to speak of "being certain that one knows" instead of "knowing that one knows." The former phrase, like the latter, is sometimes taken (for reasons which I shall not discuss here) to indicate that the speaker is using the verb *know* in its full (fullest) sense. "Being certain that one knows" may also be taken, however, to mean "feeling sure that one knows." Here we fall back to a sense of (63) which is not only different from (63)₂ but from (63)₁ and (63)₃ as well. We have met it before in the form of (63)₀. The subjective sense of certainty which it employs ought to be, but has not always been, distinguished from the "objective" senses of certainty. This ambiguity of the word "certain" (and of its

---

[27] If the question had been, "Are you *certain* that you know?", the patient could have answered "Yes" merely because he *felt* certain. Not so with the question, "Do you *know* that you know?"

cognates) makes it particularly easy to confuse the two interpretations $(63)_0$ and $(63)_2$ of (63).

5.9. *The choice between the residual meanings.*

One's choice between the different residual meanings can sometimes be predicted. A psychologist may be expected to be primarily interested in knowledge as awareness. More interestingly, one of the residual meanings is much more natural than the others in first-person sentences. It has already been pointed out (in section 5.5) that the difference between "I know" and "I know that I know" cannot very well lie in my actually following the implications of my knowledge in one case but not in the other. Neither is it natural to construe knowledge as awareness here; saying "I know that p but I am not aware that I know" is patently self-defeating. Hence there remains only the interpretation of "I know that I know" as "I am certain I know" (in either of the two senses of this phrase). It is less unnatural to say "I think that the information I have amounts to knowledge, but I am not certain that it does" than to construe "I know but I don't know that I know" in any of the other ways we have met.

This peculiarity of first-person sentences may also explain why philosophers, self-conscious as they are about the facts of knowledge, have frequently been preoccupied with the interpretation of "knowing that one knows" as "being certain that one knows": they have taken the first-person uses as a paradigm.

This cannot be the whole story, however. If philosophers like Spinoza or Prichard accepted this sense of "knowing that one knows," why did they hold that it is implied by knowing *simpliciter?* (Accepting any residual meaning presupposes that the implication breaks down.) Again logic suggests an informed guess. Philosophers are concerned not only with their own knowledge but also with the question whether claims to knowledge are really justified by the grounds the claimant has. In other words, they are interested in the (normal) sense of knowledge which satisfies (A.PKK*) and (C.KK*). And these suffice —if we abstract from the problems caused by (C.~K)—to prove the (virtual) equivalence of "knowing" to "knowing that one knows." This may explain why philosophers have so frequently accepted the equivalence.

It also throws further light on Spinoza's and Prichard's fallacy. It is not unnatural for philosophers to express their preoccupation with the justification of knowledge by saying that they are concerned with the *certainty* of our knowledge. This reinforces the tendency, already insinuated into their thinking by the preoccupation with their own knowledge, to interpret "knowing that one knows" as "being certain that one knows." It has already been pointed out that the fallacy of Spinoza and Prichard consists in confusing the two senses $(63)_0$ and $(63)_2$ of (63). It was also pointed out that these two senses are particularly easy to confuse because they may be expressed by one and the same form of words, namely, "*a* is certain that he knows that *p*." Now we see, furthermore, that a philosopher's professional interests make it very natural for him to read (63) in this very way. In short, we must admit, it seems to me, that the mistake of Spinoza and Prichard is very tempting (not to say predictable), given their interests. Perhaps this is why it has been committed repeatedly in the history of philosophy.[28]

Why is the difficulty of driving a wedge between "I know" and "I know that I know" peculiar to first-person sentences? (Even "I know that *p* but I am not certain that I do" is definitely more unnatural than "He knows that *p* but is not certain that he does.") The general reason lies in the fact that "I know" implies "I know that I know" epistemically. This, in brief, is

---

[28] Perusal of relevant literature would easily reveal more cases in point.

what my remarks amounted to when I pointed out that asserting the former while denying the latter is "self-defeating" (cf. also section 5.5 above).[29] It is interesting to see that the presence or absence of epistemic implications makes a difference even when they obtain (or fail to obtain) between virtually equivalent sentences. This fact graphically shows that one's intuitions about logical relationships are likely to be conglomerations of implications of many different kinds, and that they must therefore be analyzed rather than trusted implicitly.

The multiplicity of the residual meanings of (63), which I do not claim to have exhausted, may not be entirely unrepresentative of the richness and fluidity of ordinary language, which has rightly been emphasized recently. Notice, however, that recognizing this multiplicity has not necessitated any changes in the relatively simple rules which are basic to our study, or diminished their importance.

5.10. *Believing that one believes.* We may also observe that the notions of knowledge and belief do not behave in the same way with respect to the repetition of the "operator" "K_a" or "B_a." It was already pointed out that

(72)   "$B_a p$"

virtually implies

(73)   "$B_a B_a p$."

The latter sentence does not, however, virtually imply the former, although the corresponding implication is trivial for "K_a." An attempt to show that (73) virtually implies (72) may proceed as follows:

---

[29] The difficulty of separating the meanings of "I know" and "I know that I know" even when knowledge is construed as awareness reflects the fact that the epistemic implication which connects the two is independent of (C.KK*) as distinguished from (C.K*). For this reason it remains valid even when (C.KK*) fails.

(74) "$B_a B_a p$" ϵ μ $\Big\}$ by assumption;

(75) "$\sim B_a p$" ϵ μ

(76) "$C_a \sim p$" ϵ μ from (75) by $(C.\sim B)$;

(77) "$\sim p$" ϵ μ^* from (76) by $(C.C^*)$;

(78) "$B_a B_a p$" ϵ μ^* from (74) by $(C.BB^*)$;

(79) "$B_a p$" ϵ μ^* from (74) by $(C.B^*)$;

(80) p ϵ μ^{**} from (79) by $(C.b^*)$;

(81) "$B_a B_a p$" ϵ μ^{**} from (78) by $(C.BB^*)$;

(82) "$B_a p$" ϵ μ^{**} from (79) by $(C.BB^*)$.

Here the result of an attempted counterexample construction really is a counterexample. If we assume that the only members of μ, μ^*, and μ^{**} are those indicated by (74)–(82), that the second is an alternative to the first (with respect to a) while the third is an alternative to the second as well as to itself, then the set (of sets) $\Omega = \{\mu,\ \mu^*,\ \mu^{**}\}$ is a model system which shows that (73) does not virtually imply (72).

I find this result agreeable to our logical intuition. It is not unnatural to say of a man that he believes that he believes although he does not in fact do so: "Some make the world believe that they believe what they do not believe. Others, in greater number, make themselves believe it." [30] These words of Montaigne pertain primarily to religious belief, but this fact does not seem to affect those properties of the notion we are now discussing. A more relevant objection would be to allege that Montaigne himself contradicts our theory, for he goes on to say: ". . . being unable to penetrate what it means to believe." This suggests that, according to Montaigne, whoever believes that

---

[30] *The Complete Works of Montaigne*, ed. by Donald M. Frame (Stanford, Calif., 1957), p. 322.

he believes what he does not in fact believe is misusing the notion of belief. In a sense, this is the case. But acknowledging this does not necessitate making (73) imply (72). Montaigne would, I presume, admit that the form of words

(83)   "*a* believes that he believes that *p* although he does not believe it"

can be used to make a true and correct statement about somebody else's beliefs. It seems to me that his suggestion is, rather, that there is something wrong about a man who says (whether aloud or "in his heart"):

(84)   "I believe that I believe that *p* although I do not believe it."

Since (83) is not indefensible, (84) is not indefensible, either. But a man who says (84) fails to penetrate what it means to believe in a subtler way: he is saying something which might be true if said by somebody else of him (in the third person) but which he cannot himself believe. In other words, although (84) is not indefensible *simpliciter*, it is *doxastically* indefensible; for although statements of the form

"$B_a B_a p$ & $\sim B_a p$"

are defensible, statements of the form

"$B_a(B_a B_a p$ & $\sim B_a p)$"

are not. In fact, even statements of the more general form

"$B_a(B_a q$ & $\sim q)$"

are indefensible, as the reader may easily verify.

Hence the objection is not irremovable: we can give a sense to Montaigne's statement without changing our theory in the least. The case he mentions is in fact one in which the failure to recognize a doxastic implication smacks of self-deception.

Six

Knowledge, Belief, and Existence

6.1. *Quantifiers in model sets.* So far we have not yet discussed the interesting problems which arise when *quantifiers* (such as "there is" and "for all") are allowed to associate with epistemic operators. Now it is time to tackle them. How can we extend the methods outlined in Chapter Three so as to include quantifiers?

If no epistemic notions were present, the task would be very easy. The following additions to our earlier discussion would serve our purposes:

a) We recognize the possibility that some of our atomic (and a fortiori nonatomic) sentences may contain *names* and other *singular terms* each purporting to refer to a well-defined object. Such terms will be represented in our symbolic notation by *free individual symbols*. (As symbols of this kind, we shall use the letters a, b, c, . . .) In addition to them, we shall need *bound individual symbols* (bound individual variables). For bound individual variables, we shall use the letters x, y, z, . . . (Since the only kind of bound variables we shall be dealing with is the bound individual variable, the word "individual" will often be omitted.)

b) The formation rules of section 1.6 are augmented by adding the following additional rules:

(*v*) If p is a formula containing occurrences of a but not those of x, then "$(Ex)p(x/a)$" and "$(Ux)p(x/a)$" are also formulas.

Here "(Ex)" and "(Ux)" are called quantifiers. They are the translations into our symbolism of the expressions "There is an individual (say x) such that" and "Every individual (say x) is such that." And $p(x/a)$ is the formula obtained from p by replacing every occurrence of a by one of x. In the formulas introduced by (*v*), $p(x/a)$ is said to be the *scope* of the quantifier in question.[1] In "$(Ex)p(x/a)$" and in "$(Ux)p(x/a)$" the occurrences of x in $p(x/a)$ are said to be *bound to* the initial quantifier.

c) The conditions which define a model set (see Chapter Three) are supplemented by the following conditions:

(C.E)   If "$(Ex)p$" ϵ μ, then $p(a/x)$ ϵ μ for at least one free individual symbol a.

(C.U)   If "$(Ux)p$" ϵ μ and if b occurs in at least one member of μ, then $p(b/x)$ ϵ μ.

(C.$\sim$E)   If "$\sim(Ex)p$" ϵ μ, then "$(Ux)\sim p$" ϵ μ.

(C.$\sim$U)   If "$\sim(Ux)p$" ϵ μ, then "$(Ex)\sim p$" ϵ μ.

If we disregard epistemic notions, the resulting system may be shown to be equivalent to the usual formulations of quantifica-

---

[1] In the sequel, p, q, r, . . . , will either be arbitrary formulas (sentences, if you want) or expressions which are like formulas (sentences) except for containing bound individual symbols in the place of some free ones.

tion theory in the sense that a formula is valid (self-sustaining) if and only if it is provable in the usual formulations. (Strictly speaking, we have to use a formulation in which empty universes of discourse are not disregarded; but this is a very minor point.) This was in effect shown in the first of my "Two Papers on Symbolic Logic." [2] Hence we need not waste our time on the details of our system.

6.2. *Eliminating existential presuppositions.* Before we consider what happens when quantifiers are allowed to associate with epistemic notions, we have to make two changes in the simple setup above in order to be able to combine the two in a natural way. Of these changes, one is trivial whereas the other is highly interesting.

The trivial change is due to the necessity of distinguishing two different kinds of (free or bound) individual symbols: on one hand those referring to (or ranging over) individuals (persons) of whom it makes sense to say that they know or fail to know something, and on the other those referring to individuals (objects) which cannot properly be said to know or to believe anything. As free and bound individual symbols of the former sort, we shall continue to use a, b, c, . . . and x, y, z, . . . , respectively. As free and bound symbols of the latter kind, we might employ i, j, k, . . . and t, u, v, . . . , respectively. Symbols of the first kind might be called free and bound *personal* symbols, symbols of the second kind *impersonal* ones. Among themselves, both kinds of individual symbols behave exactly in the same way. It is therefore unnecessary to write out the analogues to (C.E)–(C.∼U) for impersonal symbols. The only difference between personal and impersonal symbols we have to observe is that the former can serve as subscripts of epistemic operators while the latter cannot.

---

[2] *Acta Philosophica Fennica*, VIII (1955).

Existence

The nontrivial change is due to the *existential presuppositions* which underlie all the traditional treatments of the quantification theory and which can be seen to underlie (C.E) and (C.U) as well. It is assumed as a rule that every free individual symbol we have to deal with really refers to some actually existing individual. Empty singular terms are disqualified as substitution-instances of individual symbols. It is obvious that this assumption is made, for example, in (C.U): from the fact that something is true of all actually existing individuals it follows that the same is true of the individual referred to by *b* only if this term really refers to some actually existing individual.[3]

These existential presuppositions may be relatively innocuous for the purposes for which quantification theory is usually developed. For the purpose of combining quantification with epistemic notions, however, they are obnoxious. We cannot accept a logic according to which "*a* believes that he is pursued by the Abominable Snowman" implies that there is such a thing as the Abominable Snowman.

How are the existential presuppositions to be avoided? We want to restrict the applicability of (C.U) to individual symbols *b* which are not empty. In other words, we want to make the applicability of (C.U) contingent on the presence of the sentence "*b* exists" in μ. How are we to translate this sentence into our symbolism? By far the best candidate seems to be "$(Ex)(x = b)$";

---

[3] Existential presuppositions are discussed in an earlier paper of mine entitled "Existential Presuppositions and Existential Commitments," *Journal of Philosophy*, LVI (1959), 125–137. The method of eliminating undesirable presuppositions which I there outlined is in principle the same as the one I am about to explain. The only difference is that the framework of model sets makes my method much easier to expound and (I hope) to appreciate. Essentially the same point has also been made independently by Hugues Leblanc and Theodore Hailperin in "Nondesignating Singular Terms," *Philosophical Review*, LXVIII (1959), 239–243.

if "*b* exists" and "There exists an individual identical with *b*" are not synonymous, what is? This explication of "*b* exists" has, moreover, the additional interest of being interpretable as an explication of Quine's famous dictum "To be is to be a value of a bound variable."

Hence we shall have to replace (C.U) by the following slightly more complicated condition:

(C.U$_0$) If "$(Ux)p$" ϵ μ and "$(Ey)(y = b)$" ϵ μ, then $p(b/x)$ ϵ μ.

Similarly, the condition (C.E) has to be changed as follows:

(C.E$_0$) If "$(Ex)p$" ϵ μ, then $p(a/x)$ ϵ μ and "$(Ex)(x = a)$" ϵ μ for at least one free individual symbol a.

Analogous conditions must of course be set up for the impersonal symbols. In (C.U$_0$) we shall disregard the difference between "(Ey) $(y=b)$" and "(Ey) $(b=y)$."

A simple example illustrates the effects of the change. By means of (C.U) we could show that p implies (virtually implies) "$(Ex)p(x/b)$" provided that b occurs in p (while x does not).[4] For if it did not, we could have

(85) p ϵ μ,

(86) "$\sim (Ex)p(x/b)$" ϵ μ

for some model set μ. This would be impossible, however, for we would have

(87) "$(Ux)\sim p(x/b)$" ϵ μ from (86) by (C.$\sim$E);

(88) "$\sim (p(x/b))(b/x)$" ϵ μ from (87) by (C.U);

---

[4] The transition from p to "$(Ex)p(x/b)$" is called *existential generalization* with respect to b in p. By "implies" we shall in this chapter mean "virtually implies," unless there are indications to the contrary.

and since $(p(x/b))(b/x)$ is here the same sentence as p, (85) and (88) would violate (C.$\sim$).

If (C.U) is replaced by (C.U$_0$), however, this argument fails, for the step from (87) to (88) becomes invalid. It can only be restored if

$$\text{``}(Ey)(y = b)\text{''} \quad \epsilon \quad \mu.$$

This means that p now implies "$(Ex)p(x/b)$" only in conjunction with "$(Ey)(y = b)$." From the fact that Moby Dick is a white whale one may infer that there exists a white whale only if Moby Dick really exists.

6.3. *Knowing who.* In the conditions (C.E$_0$) and (C.U$_0$) the notion of identity was used. One of the tasks confronting us is to decide what conditions this notion is subject to.

Before trying to do so, however, it might be useful to have a look at some of the ways in which quantifiers may be useful in analyzing constructions containing the verb *know*. Some constructions of this kind are so familiar that once we have mastered them they will help us to deal with the further problems into which we shall run.

Among the most familiar constructions with the verb *know* there are the locutions "knows who," "knows what," "knows when," "knows where," and the like. All of these are easy to translate into our symbolism; as it happens, the first is the easiest of all, for we happen to have special variables ranging over human beings. Under what circumstances is it true to say of you, with respect to a certain property, "He knows who has this property"? For example, when is it true to say of you, "He knows who is the murderer of Toto de Brunel"? [5] Clearly you know this only if you know a right answer to the question: Who killed

---

[5] With an apology to Lawrence Durrell for taking the name of one of his characters in vain.

Toto? And this you can do only if there is someone of whom you know that he (or she) killed Toto. The translation of "*a* knows who killed Toto" into our symbolism is therefore "$(Ex)K_a(x$ killed Toto)." In general, *a* knows who has the attribute defined by the expression *p* (which contains the variable *x*) if and only if the sentence

"$(Ex)K_ap$"

is true. This sentence therefore constitutes a translation of the sentence "*a* knows who is such that *p*."

If we had at our disposal special kinds of variables ranging over moments of time or over locations in space, we should be able to analyze the locutions "knows when" and "knows where" in a completely analogous fashion. Since we do not have them and since we shall not have any use of them in this work, we may content ourselves with introducing the special predicates "$T(u)$," read "*u* is a moment of time," and "$L(u)$," read "*u* is a location in space." Then we may (as a rule) translate the sentence "*a* knows when *p*" by "$(Eu)(T(u)$ & $K_a(p$ at *u*))" and the sentence "*a* knows where *b* is" by "$(Eu)(L(u)$ & $K_a(b$ is in *u*))." Similar constructions may be dealt with similarly.

I have chosen to disregard the presupposition of *uniqueness* which often seems to underlie questions asked in terms of "who," "when," "where," and the like as well as statements made in terms of "knows who," "knows when," "knows where," and the like. It seems to me that this presupposition is not always made; hence it does not seem necessary to incorporate it in our translations. And even if it were made, the changes it would necessitate in our subsequent discussion would only add to the complexity of our discussion but not alter it substantially.

6.4. *Identity in model systems.* The concept of identity may be brought within the scope of our methods by stipulating that, for any free individual symbols a and b, "$a = b$" is to be a formula (its negation may be written "$a \neq b$"), and by adopting the following additional conditions to be satisfied by all model sets:

(C. =) If $p \ \epsilon \ \mu$, "$a = b$" $\epsilon \ \mu$, if p is an atomic formula or an identity, and if q is like p except that a and b have been interchanged in one or several places, then $q \ \epsilon \ \mu$;

(C.self$\neq$) For no free individual symbol a, "$a \neq a$" $\epsilon \ \mu$.

These conditions must of course be also satisfied by free individual symbols of the other kind. The "and if" clause of (C. =) may be expressed more succinctly as follows: 'and if $p \ (a/b)$ is the same formula as $q(a/b)$.'

Instead of (C.self$\neq$) it is often advisable to use the following equivalent condition:[6]

(C.self=) If a occurs in the formulas of μ, "$a = a$" $\epsilon \ \mu$.

All the three conditions (C. =), (C.self$\neq$), and (C.self=) seem to me so obvious as to need no apology.

The rationale of the following pair of conditions:

(C. = K) If "$K_a p$" $\epsilon \ \mu$ and "$a = b$" $\epsilon \ \mu$, then "$K_b p$" $\epsilon \ \mu$;

(C. = P) If "$P_a p$" $\epsilon \ \mu$ and "$a = b$" $\epsilon \ \mu$, then "$P_b p$" $\epsilon \ \mu$;

should be equally obvious: what a man knows or does not know does not depend on how he is being referred to.

The restriction to atomic formulas and identities in (C. =) may be loosened somewhat by merely requiring that a and b must not occur within the scope of an epistemic operator in p or

---

[6] Conditions which define a model set or a model system are said to be equivalent if the choice between them does not affect the notions of defensibility, self-sustenance, virtual implication, and the like.

in q. The resulting stronger condition can be shown to follow from the original form of $(C.=)$ (together with the conditions adopted in Chapter Three) by a simple argument which proceeds by induction on the total number of symbols $\sim$, &, v, E, U in p.

The condition $(C.=)$ cannot be extended, however, to cases in which a or b occurs within the scope of an epistemic operator. If the restriction to atomic formulas were simply removed from $(C.=)$—we shall call the resulting condition $(C.=!)$—we would have to say that anyone who knows (or believes) that Mr. Hyde is a murderer also knows (or believes) that Dr. Jekyll is a murderer even if he does not know that the two are identical, solely because they are in fact identical. For then "$K_a p$" and "$b = c$" would (when conjoined) virtually imply "$K_a q$" for every q for which $p(b/c)$ and $q(b/c)$ are one and the same sentence. This, clearly, is not the way in which we normally use the verbs *know* and *believe*.

Of course, if the identity were known to the person referred to by a, the situation would be completely different. It is easily seen that "$K_a p$" and "$K_a(b = c)$" together virtually imply "$K_a q$" if $p(b/c)$ is the same formula as $q(b/c)$ and if neither of them contains epistemic operators. An argument to this effect might run as follows:

(89)	"$K_a p$" ϵ μ	
(90)	"$K_a(b = c)$" ϵ μ	counterassumption;
(91)	"$\sim K_a q$" ϵ μ	
(92)	"$P_a \sim q$" ϵ μ	from (91) by $(C.\sim K)$;
(93)	"$\sim q$" ϵ μ^*	from (92) by $(C.P^*)$;
(94)	p ϵ μ^*	from (89) by $(C.K^*)$;
(95)	"$b = c$" ϵ μ^*	from (90) by $(C.K^*)$;
(96)	q ϵ μ^*	from (94) and (95) by an extension of $(C.=)$.

Here (93) and (96) constitute a violation of (C.∼), thus proving the desired virtual implication by a *reductio ad absurdum*. If we had had instead of (90) merely "$b = c$" ϵ μ, the step (95) would be invalid, and no virtual implication would be forthcoming.

This example is generalizable in interesting ways. If we disregard B and C for the time being, we can prove the following generalization:

(97)   "p & $K_a(b = c)$" virtually implies q if $p(b/c)$ is the same formula as $q(b/c)$ and if all the epistemic operators in p and q have the subscript a.

This can be proved if it can be proved that p, "$K_a(b = c)$," and "$\sim q$" cannot belong to one and the same member μ of a model system under the assumptions of (97). We shall not prove this in detail here, but we shall show how it can be proved. It can be proved by induction on the number of the symbols '∼,' '&,' 'v,' 'E,' 'U,' 'K,' and 'P' in p (or in q, which is seen to yield the same number). A basis for induction is obtained by considering the case in which this number is zero. In this case we obtain the desired result by (C. =) and (C.K). The inductive step falls into several cases according to the form of the formula p. Most of these cases are trivial. In the case in which p is of the form "$K_a p_1$" the argument proceeds in the same way as in (89)–(96) up to (94) except that p is replaced by p_1. Instead of (95) we may put

"$K_a(b = c)$" ϵ μ^* from (90) by (C.KK*),

and instead of (96) we may use the inductive hypothesis to establish the desired conclusion. The case in which p is of the form "$P_a p_1$" is closely similar.

This suffices to show how (97) can be proved. It can be generalized in various ways to cases in which more than one free individual symbol may occur as the subscript of an epistemic operator in p. We shall not go into the details of these generalizations, however. Broadly speaking, they show that the restriction to atomic formulas can be eliminated from (C. =) provided we strengthen the premises of this condition to say not only that certain identities in fact hold but that they are also *known* to hold. In some cases, premises of the form "$K_a(b = c)$" ϵ μ do the trick; in some others, we need premises of the form "(Ux) $K_x(b = c)$" ϵ μ, or even of the form "$K_{a_1}K_{a_2} \ldots K_{a_k}(b = c)$" ϵ μ.

Broadly speaking, assumptions of the kind exemplified by (90) therefore enable us to strengthen (C. =) to (C. = !). This may be seen in another way, too. It may be shown that the system obtained by strengthening (C. =) to (C. = !) is equivalent, as far as the notions of defensibility, self-sustenance, virtual implication, and the like are concerned, to a system obtained by adopting the following requirement:

(C.K =) If "$b = c$" ϵ μ, then "$K_a(b = c)$" ϵ μ.

(This is supposed to hold for every a, b, and c, of course.) This fact (which we shall not prove here) graphically shows that the assumption which underlies (C. = !) is illicit: it amounts to assuming that everybody knows the answers (right answers) to all questions of identity.

This fact is interesting because (C. = !) is the exact formulation within our approach of what has been called the principle of the *substitutivity of identity*. Sometimes this principle seems to have been thought of as being beyond any reasonable doubt. What we have seen shows that, on the contrary, it is in epistemic contexts obviously invalid, for it is equivalent to an assumption which is clearly false.

6.5. *The influence of epistemic implications.* The situation is some-what complicated by the fact that although "$K_a p$" and "$b = c$" do not virtually imply "$K_a q$" always when $p(b/c) = q(b/c)$, the first two imply the third *epistemically* when uttered by the person referred to by a. In other words, the sentence "$K_a(K_a p \ \& \ (b = c) \ \& \ \sim K_a q)$" is indefensible if $p(b/c) = q(b/c)$. In fact, if we make the counterassumption:

(98)   "$K_a(K_a p \ \& \ (b = c) \ \& \ \sim K_a q)$" ϵ μ,

we may obtain (89) and (91) by (C.K) and (C.&). From these we may obtain (92)–(94) as before. We cannot get (95) from (90), but we may obtain it by way of

(99)   "$K_a p \ \& \ (b = c) \ \& \ \sim K_a q$" ϵ μ^* from (98) by (C.K*).

Then (95) is yielded by (99) in virtue of (C.&), and the rest goes as before.

By making a slight change we could even replace "$K_a p$" by "$K_d p$" in this argument (for an arbitrary d).

It is not impossible that recent discussion of the principle of substitutivity of identity in epistemic contexts has been influenced by a confusion between the different implications. In many typical cases, a putative implication which is invalid as a virtual implication but which would be valid if (C. = !) were acceptable turns out to be justifiable after all when interpreted as an epistemic (or doxastic) implication. This may have been instrumental in leading people to think that (C. = !) is applicable more widely than it really is. They are mistaken, however, in taking this to support (C. = !); the correct epistemic or doxastic implications which lie at the bottom of their intuitions must of course be based on (C. =) and not on the incorrect condition (C. = !). It is true that a man who says "I know that p" (or sometimes even "*a* knows that *p*") and adds "*b* is the same person as *c*" may often be expected to conclude "I know that *q*" (when $p(b/c)$ and $q(b/c)$ are one and the same sentence). This was not denied, however, when we denied the principle of substitutivity of identity. We may explain the transition from the first two to the third in terms of an epistemic implication holding between them. In order to bring out the import of our denial of the principle it is fairer to consider the corresponding third-person sentences, and to think of them as uttered by somebody whose knowledge is not being discussed.

6.6 *Referential opacity as referential multiplicity.* Contexts in which the substitutivity of identity holds W. V. O. Quine calls *referentially transparent;* contexts in which it fails he calls *referentially opaque.* The reasons for the referential opacity of certain contexts and the difficulties which one encounters when one tries to *quantify into* such a context—i.e., to replace a free individual symbol occurring in such a context by an individual variable which is bound to a quantifier outside—have recently given rise to a great deal of comment. It seems to me that some light can be thrown on these questions by means of our methods.

Trying to keep as close to our common-sense view of the matter as possible, let us ask: Why does it not follow from "*a* knows that Mr. Hyde is a murderer" and "Dr. Jekyll is the same man as Mr. Hyde" that the person referred to by *a* knows that Dr. Jekyll is murderer? The obvious, and trivial, answer is that he may not *know* that the two are identical. But what exactly is implied in this answer? It seems to me that the most instructive way of elaborating it is as follows: In so far as the person referred to by *a* does not know everything there is to be known about the world he has to keep an eye on more than one "possible world," that is, he has to take into account more than one way things might actually be, as far as he knows. It is obvious that this notion of a "possible world" is an innocuous one; each of us constantly makes preparations for more than one possible way things might turn out, as far as he happens to know.

Among other things, the person referred to by *a* will have to keep an eye on the different ways in which names (and other individual terms) might refer to different individuals and perhaps sometimes might fail to refer altogether. If he does not know that Dr. Jekyll and Mr. Hyde are identical, he will have to heed the possibility that they might refer to different men. To put this in a slightly different way, at least one of the "possible worlds" he will have to consider is then such that the two names refer in it to different men. When we are discussing what the person referred to by *a* knows we may always substitute a term (say "Dr. Jekyll") for another (say "Mr. Hyde") if and only if they refer to one and the same individual (if any) in *all* the "possible worlds" compatible with what he knows. But this is clearly tantamount to saying that the two terms are interchangeable if (and only if) the person in question *knows* that they refer to one and the same person, just as we found in (97).

Seen in this light, the failure of referential transparency in epistemic contexts is due to the possibility that two names or other singular terms which *de facto* refer to one and the same object (or person) are not known (or believed) by someone to do so and that they will therefore refer to different objects (or persons) in some of the "possible worlds" we have to discuss (explicitly or implicitly) in order to discuss what he knows or believes and what he does not. The referential opacity is not due here to anything strange happening to the ways in which our singular terms refer to objects nor to anything unusual about the objects to which they purport to refer. It is simply and solely due to the fact that we have to consider more than one way in which they could refer (or fail to refer) to objects. What we have to deal with here is therefore not so much a failure of referentiality as a kind of *multiple referentiality*.[7]

Our approach is calculated to bring out this fact. The model sets which are epistemic alternatives to a given model set μ (with respect to a) may be thought of as descriptions of states of affairs compatible with all that the person referred to by a knows in the state of affairs described by μ. The multiplicity of epistemic alternatives reflects the multiplicity of states of affairs compatible with what he knows. The fact that some identities may hold in one model set but not in others reflects the fact that our singular terms might refer to objects in different ways in the different states of affairs in question. The fact that within each such state of affairs ("possible world") our terms refer to objects in a normal way is indicated by the fact that (C. =) is valid and that it can be extended to cover all the occurrences of free individual symbols outside epistemic operators. This condition may be thought of as saying that two terms which in a certain state of affairs refer to identical objects are interchangeable as far as that particular state of affairs is concerned. For new "possible worlds" are introduced by epistemic operators and only by them; hence occurrences of terms outside epistemic operators in the sentences of a model set μ speak only of the state of affairs described by μ.

The informal explanation which I gave for the failure of "a knows that Mr. Hyde is a murderer" and "Dr. Jekyll = Mr. Hyde" to imply "a knows that Dr. Jekyll is a murderer" is also accurately reflected by our formal treatment. The reason for the failure is the same as the reason why the argument (89)–(96) becomes irreparably invalid when (90) is replaced by "b = c"

---

[7] Cf. my paper "Modality as Referential Multiplicity," *Ajatus*, XX (1957), 49–64. Although I now could considerably improve on that paper, the general outlook I proposed there is the same as the one I am arguing for here.

ϵ μ. And this reason is simply that we cannot then have "$b =$ c" ϵ μ^*, that is, we cannot any more identify the persons referred by by b and by c in one of the possible states of affairs (namely, that described by μ^*) which we have to consider in order to bring out what the person referred to by a knows and what he does not know.

6.7. *The necessity of quantifying into opaque contexts.* If this diagnosis is correct, we may expect no difficulties in combining quantification with epistemic operators as long as we merely quantify over individuals existing within some particular "possible world." As we said, new "possible worlds" are introduced into our arguments by epistemic operators and only by them; hence this simple case may be described formally by saying that in it each quantifier and all the occurrences of the variable bound to it occur within the scope of exactly the same epistemic operators. In other words, in the formation rules for existential and universal quantification (cf. section 6.1) we should stipulate that none of the occurrences of a in p may be within the scope of an epistemic operator. This is the exact meaning of the prohibition to quantify into a context governed by an epistemic operator.

It is generally agreed that this case is in fact unproblematic. Quantifiers and epistemic operators mix easily as long as we do not quantify across epistemic operators.

This simple case does not suffice, however, for our treatment of epistemic notions *cum* quantification. There are perfectly ordinary expressions whose explication is possible only in terms of quantifiers which bind variables occurring beyond the boundary of epistemic operators. The expressions "knows who," "knows where," and the like discussed in 6.3 are cases in point. The difference between "a knows who the dictator of Portugal is" and "a knows that there is a dictator of Portugal" (more idiomatically, "*a* knows that Portugal is a dictatorship"), in short, the difference between

(100)   "$(Ex)K_a$(the dictator of Portugal $= x$)"

and

(101)   "$K_a(Ex)$(the dictator of Portugal $= x$)"

illustrates the distinction involved. There are no problems worth discussing here about the meaning of (101) but there are intriguing problems about sentences of the form (100) which have recently given philosophers of logic a great deal of thought.

W. V. O. Quine has taken the view that quantification into a referentially opaque neighborhood is always misguided.[8] Since in sentences like (100) we undeniably quantify into contexts governed by epistemic operators, he has maintained that contexts governed by such operators are sometimes construed transparently and that they are always construed transparently when they are quantified into. In other words, he admits of (at least) two senses of each epistemic operator, a transparent sense and an opaque sense. For instance, according to Quine the sentence

(102)   "*a* knows that the dictator of Portugal is Dr. Salazar"

admits of two interpretations, a transparent one and an opaque one. On the transparent interpretation, (102) is implied by any sentence of the form

"*a* knows that the dictator of Portugal is *b*"

together with the simple identity "*b* = Dr. Salazar." For instance, (102) is implied by

(103)   "*a* knows that the dictator of Portugal is the dictator of Portugal."

---

[8] See his *Word and Object* (New York, 1960); "Quantification and Propositional Attitudes," *Journal of Philosophy*, LIII (1956), 177–187; *From a Logical Point of View* (Cambridge, Mass., 1953).

Normally, we have an option between the two interpretations of (102). But in case we want to generalize existentially with respect to "Dr. Salazar," we must use the transparent interpretation.

This view of Quine's may, however, be shown to be unsatisfactory provided that we accept the analysis of the phrase "knows who" which was outlined in section 6.3. It may be shown to force us to accept statements of the form "*a* knows who . . ." as true which are clearly false according to our normal lights. In our example, (103) is true as soon as the person referred to by *a* knows that Portugal is a dictatorship. Since (102), transparently interpreted, is implied by (103), it must also be true as soon as (103) is true even if our man does not have any idea of the name or of the other attributes of Portugal's strongman. This may seem disconcerting, but it can probably be explained away as a curious by-product of the duality of interpretations; what is true on one interpretation need not be true on the other. What is unacceptable is that (100) is implied by (102) and therefore also by (103), transparently interpreted. Since the last one is trivially true, the first one must be trivially true, too. It follows that no one can help knowing who Portugal's dictator is as soon as one knows that Portugal is a dictatorship. The duality of interpretations does not help us any longer, for there is no such duality to avail ourselves of here. According to Quine, existential generalization with respect to a term is possible only when the term occurs in a transparent context. Accordingly, the epistemic operator of (100) must be interpreted transparently. But then (100) is implied by (103) as well as by (102), transparently interpreted, exactly as we feared.

Since I cannot find any fault with our analysis of the phrase "knows who" in 6.3, I conclude that something must be wrong with Quine's views. This is also suggested by the fact that we can construct similar counterexamples which are not in terms of the locution "knows who." The sentence "There is nobody whom the police so far suspect of yesterday's bank robbery" is a perfectly ordinary sentence which seems to be equivalent to "There is nobody in particular whom the police so far believe to have committed yesterday's bank robbery" and which can certainly be true although the police believe that the bank was robbed by the man who was seen driving to the bank in a gray sedan. (They do not know who this man was nor have they any opinions on the matter.) Suppose that this man in fact was Ben the Burglar, an old customer of the police, although they do not yet suspect him. In spite of their unawareness, Quine would be forced to say that, in the sense in which the sentence can be generalized existentially, the police believe that the bank was robbed by Ben and that there hence exists a man of whom the police believe that he robbed the bank yesterday.

6.8. *The prerequisites for quantifying into opaque contexts.* It is usually easier to criticize others than to make constructive suggestions. It would be fair, then, if you do not give full credit to my criticism of Quine's theory unless and until I improve on it.

Although I cannot accept Quine's solution, the problems he is dealing with are interesting and difficult. My own tentative solution is suggested by an examination of the apparently simple form of words "*a* knows who Dr. Salazar is." Simplicity notwithstanding, this sentence is perplexing. On one hand, it seems to be analyzable as

(104) "$(Ex)K_a(\text{Dr. Salazar} = x)$";

on the other, this analysis seems unsatisfactory in that (104) is apparently implied by

(105) "$K_a(\text{Dr. Salazar} = \text{Dr. Salazar})$,"

which can scarcely fail to be true, provided that *a* knows that

Dr. Salazar exists. It seems to follow that no one who knows that Dr. Salazar exists can fail to know who he is.

Our predicament here is not unlike the predicaments in which we are likely to find ourselves if we do not give up the existential presuppositions which are usually made in quantification theory (cf. section 6.2). On one hand, "Pegasus exists" seems to be analyzable as

(106)   "(Ex)(Pegasus $= x$)";

on the other, this analysis seems unsatisfactory in that (106) is apparently implied by

(107)   "(Pegasus $=$ Pegasus),"

which can scarcely fail to be true. It seems to follow that Pegasus cannot fail to exist.

The solution I shall suggest to our present problem is similar to the solution we gave to the problem of Pegasus' existence. The implication from (107) to (106) turns on the condition (C.U), that is, on substituting "Pegasus" for a universally bound individual variable. The solution consisted in prohibiting substitution of this kind unless we have as an extra premise the sentence "Pegasus exists," formally "(Ex)(Pegasus $= x$)." In the particular case at hand, this was the very sentence we wanted to deduce from (106). The alleged implication is therefore a *petitio principii*. Formally, our solution amounts to replacing (C.E) and (C.U) by (C.E$_0$) and (C.U$_0$).

Similarly, we may observe that the alleged implication from (105) to (104) turns on substituting "Dr. Salazar" for a universally bound variable which occurs both within and without the scope of an epistemic operator with a as a subscript. Our problems are dissolved, it seems to me, if we simply prohibit a substitution of this kind unless we have an additional premise of the form "a knows who Dr. Salazar is," formally (104). In the particular case at hand, this was the very sentence we wanted to deduce from (105). The alleged implication therefore begs the question.

Formally speaking, my suggestion amounts in this simple case to using, instead of (C.E$_o$) and (C.U$_o$), the following simple conditions:

(108) If "$(Ex)p$" ϵ μ, then for at least one free individual symbol a we have $p(a/x)$ ϵ μ and "$(Ex)K_b(a = x)$" ϵ μ, provided that there are in p no epistemic operators different from "K_b" and "P_b" and that x occurs within the scope of one of them in p.

(109) If "$(Ux)p$" ϵ μ and "$(Ey)K_b(a = y)$" ϵ μ, then $p(a/x)$ ϵ μ, provided that there are in p no epistemic operators different from "K_b" and "P_b."

As you may see, these conditions are far from general. How are we to generalize them so as to omit the "provided"-clauses? It is not very difficult to see how full generalizations may be reached. Formulating them explicitly will, however, turn out to be a rather tedious business. For our purposes in this work it suffices to confine our attention to a particular case, namely, to that in which no bound variables occur as subscripts to epistemic operators. In this section we shall generalize (108) and (109) for this case. The resulting partial generalizations will be called (C.E$_{ep}$) and (C.U$_{ep}$).

Let us first address ourselves to the problem of generalizing (108). In (C.E$_{ep}$), the role which in (108) was played by the formula "$(Ex)K_b(a = x)$" is now played by a number of formulas (we shall call them *auxiliary formulas* of p with respect to x), one for each occurrence of x in p. (The presence of "$(Ex)p$" in μ will entail the presence of all of them in μ.) Each occurrence of x in p corresponds to a sequence of epistemic operators, namely, to the sequence of those operators in the scope of which it happens, in their natural order. (The larger the scope of an operator, the earlier it therefore occurs in the sequence.) Each sequence is "reduced" by first replacing 'P' and 'C' by 'K' and 'B,' respectively, and by subsequently omitting each occurrence of an operator K or B which is immediately followed by an occurrence of the *same* operator furnished *with the same subscript*. To each such reduced sequence of operators (with subscripts), we construct an auxiliary formula by inserting it into the blank of the following schema:

"(Ex) —— $(a = x)$."

For instance, if the sequence is empty, the corresponding formula will be "$(Ex)(a = x)$," which we shall usually replace by "$(Ex)(x = a)$." If the sequence is "$K_b B_c$," the corresponding auxiliary formula is "$(Ex)K_b B_c(a = x)$"; and so on.

This suffices to indicate how the auxiliary formulas used in (C.E$_{ep}$) are to be found, that is, how (C.E$_{ep}$) is to be formulated. In (C.U$_{ep}$) the role which in (109) was played by "$(Ex)K_b(a = x)$" is now likewise played by a set of formulas which includes each auxiliary formula of p with respect to x or at least one of the *variants* of this auxiliary formula. The presence of all the members of some such set in μ is required as a premise in (C.U$_{ep}$). A formula is said to be a variant of an auxiliary formula if and only if it is like this formula except for the choice of the bound variable and for the relative positions of x and a.

Analogues to (C.E$_{ep}$) and (C.U$_{ep}$) must of course be assumed to hold for impersonal variables, too.

It is seen that (C.E$_o$) and (C.U$_o$) remain valid for the case in which p contains no epistemic operators.

It is seen that the partial generalizations (C.E$_{ep}$) and (C.U$_{ep}$) of (C.E) and (C.U) are already somewhat complicated. The appearance of complexity is no doubt heightened by the fact that I have presented the generalization very dogmatically. What is more important than the details of the generalization, however, is the question whether our approach is correct and perhaps even indispensable in the simple cases from which every generalization must start and with which we normally have to deal. What is there to be said in favor of modifying (C.E$_o$) and (C.U$_o$) along these lines?

6.9. *The prerequisites for knowing who.* For certain simple but important cases the naturalness of our solution may perhaps be seen as follows. When is it true to say "*a* knows who *b* is"? Clearly a necessary condition is that the person referred to by *a* should be able to give a right answer to the question "Who is *b*?" and that he should know that his answer is right. This necessary condition is not a sufficient one, however. Any correct and informed answer to the question "Who is *b*?" does not show that the answerer really knows to whom the term *b* refers; nor does such an answer always suffice to let the questioner know it. If you ask me "Who was the teacher of Antisthenes?" and I reply "The teacher of Antisthenes was the same man as the teacher of Aristippus," my answer does not necessarily help you to know who the teacher of Antisthenes was, for you may fail to know who the teacher of Aristippus was. Similarly, it is conceivable that my answer should not even show that I know who the former was; for I might likewise fail to know who the latter was, although I happen to know that the two are identical. (For a similar reason, it is still less helpful of me to reply: "The teacher of Antisthenes was the teacher of Antisthenes," although there is no doubt that I know this answer to be true.) The answer "The teacher of Antisthenes was the same man as the teacher of Plato" is a much better one just because it is ever so much unlikelier that you (or I) should be ignorant of who the latter was. The moral of these examples is clear: a sentence of the form "*a* knows that *b* is *c*" does not imply "*a* knows who *b* is" except in conjunction with the further premise "*a* knows who *c* is." Formally: "$K_a(b = c)$" implies "$(Ex)K_a(b = x)$" only in conjunction with the further premise "$(Ex)K_a(c = x)$." And this is exactly what our solution amounts to in this simple case.[9]

It is not difficult to see that similar remarks pertain to all sentences of the form "$(Ex)K_a p$." This sentence is implied by "$K_a p(b/x)$" only when the latter is conjoined with "$(Ex)K_a(b = x)$." Watson cannot really be said to know who has committed the latest murder even if he does know that it was committed by Mr. Hyde if he fails to know who this mysterious Mr. Hyde is.

Nor is the naturalness of our solution limited to locutions like "knows who." In fact, we anticipated our solution in the last example of 6.7 when we explained why the police cannot be said to have any suspects yet although they believe that yesterday's bank robbery was committed by the man who drove to the bank in a gray sedan: the police do not yet have any opinions as to his identity. This is exactly what our suggestions amount to in this case. If we are right, "$(Ex)B_a p$" is implied by "$B_a p(b/x)$ & $(Ex)B_a(b = x)$" but not by "$B_a p(b/x)$" alone.

---

[9] In practice it is frequently difficult to tell whether a given sentence of the form "*a* knows who *b* is" or "$(Ex)K_a(b = x)$" is true or not. The criteria as to when one may be said to know who this or that man is are highly variable. Sometimes knowing the name of the person in question suffices; sometimes it does not. Often "acquaintance" of some sort is required. Our discussion is independent of this difficulty, however. We have decided to study sets of statements only when all their members are logically comparable with each other (cf. sec. 1.3). This presupposes that one and the same set of criteria is used to decide their truth or falsity. What we are saying in the present section thus amounts to no more than this: No matter how the criteria for the truth of statements of the form "$(Ex)K_a(x = b)$" are chosen (within the limits of our normal logic), the truth of the two statements "$(Ex)K_a(x = c)$" and "$K_a(b = c)$" according to these criteria entails the truth of "$(Ex)K_a(x = b)$" according to the *same* criteria; whereas the truth of the second alone does not always suffice to entail the truth of the third.

Both the replacement of (C.E) and (C.U) by (C.E$_o$) and (C.U$_o$), respectively, and the replacement of the latter two by (C.E$_{ep}$) and (C.U$_{ep}$), respectively, involves the recognition of what may be called a logical *conservation principle*. After the former change no existential sentence is implied by sentences at least one of which does not contain a quantifier.[10] After the latter change no sentence in which a bound variable occurs within the scope of one of the epistemic operators 'K' and 'P' will be implied by sentences at least one of which does not have this property. These facts may be thought of as formalizations of the rough intuitive principles that an existential conclusion can be drawn only from premises at least one of which is also existential (explicitly or implicitly) and that a conclusion in which the identity of at least one individual is assumed to be known can be drawn only from premises at least one of which embodies the same assumption. As such, they are analogous to such earlier "conservation principles" as, for example, the principle that a normative conclusion can be drawn only from premises at least one of which is also normative.

6.10. *The prerequisites as requirements of uniqueness.* Our solution seems to remove the general theoretical difficulties recently discussed by Quine and by others which have beset attempts to combine quantification and epistemic operators. The only kind of quantification with which we are concerned here and with which we have to do in ordinary discourse is quantification over ordinary "extensional" objects, for example, over men or things or places. Now this kind of quantification is often thought of

---

[10] If only such negation-signs are assumed to be present as are immediately followed by atomic formulas, we can say "existential quantifier" instead of "quantifier." Every formula can easily be brought to a form in which this assumption is satisfied by certain trivial transformations, such as the elimination of double negations, the applications of De Morgan's laws, the interchange of "$\sim(Ex)$" and "$(Ux)\sim$," etc.

as being difficult to combine with epistemic notions because sentences containing epistemic operators do not seem to establish genuine relations between suitable objects at all. Suppose that we accept, as we have done, an interpretation of epistemic operators (the opaque one) on which the sentences

(110)   "Watson knows that Mr. Hyde is a murderer"

and

(111)   "Watson does not know that Dr. Jekyll is a murderer"

are both true although Dr. Jekyll and Mr. Hyde are in fact one and the same man. Then we have apparently ceased to affirm any relationship between Watson and any man at all. For who is the man of whom (110) is true in relation to Watson? If he is Mr. Hyde, he is *de facto* also Dr. Jekyll. But (110) is false of Dr. Jekyll, as shown by (111). In Quine's words, (110) and (111) are not, as wholes, about Dr. Jekyll or Mr. Hyde at all. For this reason, according to Quine, it is illicit to quantify into either of them. From a sentence which is not, strictly speaking, about anyone, it is impossible to obtain a sentence which is in terms of "someone." For instance, (110) cannot (if Quine is right) be generalized existentially so as to yield

(112)   "There is someone who is known by Watson to be a murderer."

What are we to make of these objections? We have already seen why (110) and (111) can both be true. Although "Dr. Jekyll" and "Mr. Hyde" in fact refer to one and the same man, they refer to different men in some of the "possible worlds" we have to discuss in order to discuss what Watson knows and does not know. For this reason, "Dr. Jekyll" and "Mr. Hyde" are not interchangeable here, and for the same reason (110) and (111) can both be true.

This line of thought now suggests a reason why we cannot always generalize existentially with respect to a term—say b—which occurs in a context where we are discussing what a certain man—let his name be a—knows and what he does not know. The term b may be such that in the different "possible worlds" which we have to heed it refers to different men. For this reason, we cannot always generalize existentially with respect to b in a sentence—say p—in which we speak about what the bearer of a knows and what he does not know. Such a p does not necessarily imply

(113)   "There is a man (say x) such that $p(x/b)$,"

for there may not be any unique individual who could serve as the appropriate value of x. The sentence p does not give us any such value, for in p the term b may not refer to any unique man at all but rather to several different men at once, qua members of the different "possible worlds"—an instance of "referential multiplicity." Hence the man it in fact refers to cannot by himself serve as the desired value of x. This is what Quine's objections seem to amount to in our terminology.

It is now easy to see a simple way of avoiding undesirable existential generalizations in epistemic contexts. Existential generalization with respect to a term—say b—is admissible in such contexts if b refers to one and the same man in all the "possible worlds" we have to consider. If we are considering what the bearer of a knows and does not know, these "possible worlds" are the states of affairs compatible with everything he knows (and compatible with everything which logically follows from what he knows). Now b clearly refers to one and the same man in all these states of affairs if there is someone who is known by the bearer of a to be referred to by b; for then there is no state of affairs compatible with what the bearer of a knows in which b should fail to refer to him. In short, b refers to one and the same man in all the "possible worlds" we have to consider in this special case if it is true to say "*a* knows who *b* is." But this is exactly what our solution amounts to here: existential generalization with respect to *b* is admissible if we have as an additional premise the sentence "*a* knows who *b* is," formally "$(Ex)K_a(b = x)$."

It may also be argued that the restriction which our solution imposes on existential generalization is in this simple case a necessary condition for its success. That it should be one is far from surprising, for Quine and others have argued that a much stronger restriction is needed. No detailed argument will therefore be given here. Suffice it to say that for the purposes of our model system technique the possibility of generalizing existentially with respect to *b* without the additional premise "$(Ex)K_a(b = x)$" is tantamount to the possibility of generalizing existentially while the negation of the premise is true. And against such a possibility we can bring to bear all the objections of Quine, transposed to our terminology and approach.

In more complicated cases, we can similarly argue that our formulations really catch the necessary and sufficient conditions for the existence of a well-defined individual referred to by a free individual term and hence also for the possibility of generalizing existentially with respect to the term. Again we shall not worry about the details here. The simple case we have discussed suffices to show, I hope, that the principal objections to quantifying into a construction governed by an epistemic operator can be met without changing the interpretation of the operator. In (C.E$_{ep}$) and (C.U$_{ep}$) we have simply been trying to state exactly when such a quantification is feasible and when it is not. Further generalizations may be obtained in the same way.

In brief, it may be said that in our view a sentence like (111) sometimes is, *pace* Quine, about Dr. Jekyll after all even when it is interpreted opaquely: (111) is about Dr. Jekyll if and only if Watson knows who Dr. Jekyll is. Then, and only then, can it be generalized existentially with respect to "Dr. Jekyll."

In our view, Quine is overcautious when he makes the referential transparency of a construction a necessary criterion for quantifying into it.[11] The transparency of a construction means, we remember, that individual terms occurring in it are subject to the substitutivity of identity. We have already seen what a term's being subject to this substitutivity amounts to in epistemic contexts: it means that all true identities with the term on one side are known (or sometimes merely believed) to be true. I do not see why this requirement should be a necessary condition for being able to quantify existentially with respect to the term. What is required for the latter purpose is uniqueness or, better, definiteness of reference: we may generalize existentially with respect to a term as soon as it really specifies an individual definite enough to serve as a value of a bound variable. It seems to me that a failure of such a specification is what Quine is really worried about, not the failure of the substitutivity of identity. If we examine his arguments, we see that he does not say that the failure of the substitutivity of identity as such makes it impossible to generalize existentially with respect to a term. (Cf. the first paragraph of this section.) Rather, he takes the failure of the substitutivity to indicate that the term in question does not refer to any bona fide individual at all, and the latter failure he takes (rightly so) to mean that existential generalization with respect to it is impossible. We are not challenging the second part of this kind of argument, but the first.

The difference between our view and Quine's may seem small, but it was already seen (in 6.7) to make all the difference

---

[11] See, e.g., *From a Logical Point of View*, p. 146. For Quine's usage of the attributes "referential" and "purely referential" in terms of which he formulates his point; cf. *Word and Object*, p. 142.

for our ability to analyze the ubiquitous locutions "knows who," "knows where," and the like.

6.11. *All men* v. *all known men*. In contexts where we are speaking of what a certain man—let his name be *a*—knows and does not know, the net effect of our solution may be said to be that all the substitution-values of a bound variable must be such that the bearer of *a* knows whom they refer to. To be more specific, this restriction affects those and only those bound variables which occur within the scope of the operators "K_a" and/or "P_a." This fact has to be kept in mind when the meaning of sentences which are couched in terms of our symbolic notation is contemplated and when they are translated into ordinary language. For instance, the sentence "$(Ux)K_ap$" really speaks of only such men as are referred to by some term of which the bearer of *a* knows whom it refers to. In a sense, it therefore speaks only of those men who are known to the bearer of *a*. Such sentences are not naturally translated into ordinary language by a sentence beginning "of each man *a* knows that"; we must rather use some locution like "of each man known to *a* he knows that." [12] (Still less can we use the phrase "*a* knows that every man" which best serves to translate "$K_a(Ux)$.")

Sometimes we may nevertheless want to say something of literally all men also when we are discussing what the bearer of *a* knows and does not know. A way of doing so is in fact provided for by our notation. In order to make it possible to substitute any name for a bound personal variable, we need only to make

---

[12] This minor inconvenience could have been avoided by assigning different roles to '*K*' and '*P*' in the conditions (C.E$_{ep}$) and (C.U$_{ep}$). The change would have entailed a considerable complication of these conditions, however, without increasing at all the extent of what we can express my means of our symbolic notation.

sure that the variable does not occur within the scope of an epistemic operator. Thus the intuitive meaning of "every man is known by a to be unhappy" (in the sense of "of each man a knows that he is unhappy," not in the sense of "a knows that every man is unhappy") is thus likely to be best expressed by "$(Ux)(Ey)(y = x$ & $K_a(y$ is unhappy))." This sentence says something of literally all men, but since it relates them to what a's bearer knows it can only speak of them as known to him under a suitable designation. Its meaning ought to be clearly distinguished from that of "$(Ux)K_a(x$ is unhappy)" on one hand and from that of "$K_a(Ux)(x$ is unhappy)" on the other.

The difference between "$(Ux)K_ap$" and "$(Ux)(Ey)(y = x$ & $K_ap(y/x))$" is strikingly shown by the fact that "$(Ux)p$" is implied by the latter but not by the former, if p contains no epistemic operators.

We shall return to these interesting distinctions. Meanwhile, it may be observed that the method by means of which we were able to express them has other uses.

One of the merits we may perhaps claim for our approach over those of Quine's is the fact that we need not postulate several irreducible senses of knowing and of believing. We have to recognize, of course, that these notions are sometimes used in Quine's transparent sense and not only in what Quine calls the opaque sense, which is the sense we have been explicating. However, for us the transparent sense is definable in terms of the basic (opaque) sense plus quantification. In fact, there is more than one way in which we can define a transparent sense in terms of the opaque one. These ways will even give slightly different results. For example, the transparent senses of "a knows that p" and "a believes that p," where p contains occurrences of the term b, could be defined as

(114)   "$(Ex)(x = b \ \& \ K_a p(x/b))$"

and

"$(Ex)(x = b \ \& \ B_a p(x/b))$"

respectively. Alternatively, we could define the transparent senses of these expressions as

(115)   "$(Ux)(x = b \supset K_a p(x/b))$"

and

"$(Ux)(x = b \supset B_a p(x/b))$"

respectively. Quine would not be able to resort to these definitions with a good conscience, of course, for they would for him either involve illicit quantification into an opaque construction (in case 'K' and 'B' are construed in the opaque sense) or else be circular (in case they are construed in the transparent sense). For us, however, they are unobjectionable.

This possibility of defining the transparent senses of knowledge and of belief within our approach may be used to show that in certain respects our results agree fairly closely with those of Quine. After having distinguished the two senses of knowledge and belief, he forbids quantification into a context governed by an epistemic operator, opaquely construed. In our approach, there is nothing to forbid us to quantify into an opaque context as little as into a transparent one. The interesting thing is that quantification into an opaque context can sometimes be proved to yield exactly the same result as quantification into the corresponding transparent construction. For instance, the sentence

"$(Ey)(Ex)(x = y \ \& \ K_a p(x/b))$"

obtained by generalizing existentially with respect to b in the transparent context (114) is virtually equivalent with the sentence

"$(Ex) K_a p(x/b)$"

obtained by generalizing existentially with respect to b in the opaque context "$K_a p$." (The proof of this virtual equivalence, though not quite short, does not involve any surprises.)

Similarly, the sentences

"$(Uy)(Ux)(x = y \supset K_a p(x/b))$"

and

"$(Ux) K_a p(x/b)$"

obtained by generalizing universally with respect to b in the sentences (115) and "$K_a p$" respectively can be shown to be virtually equivalent.

In general, it may be said that as long as we limit our attention to sentences containing just one initial epistemic operator we may replace each quantification into an opaque construction by a quantification into a suitable transparent construction. What Quine obtains by an *ad hoc* prohibition to quantify into an opaque construction is here obtained more economically as a necessary consequence of our general approach: even if we allow quantification into an opaque construction, the result does not differ from that of quantifying into a suitable transparent construction. Of course, this holds only for sentences of the simple sort we have been discussing. To judge from his examples, however, such simple contexts are what Quine has uppermost in his mind.

6.12. *The condition* (C.KK*) *qualified.* The methods developed in this chapter enable us to formulate the qualification to which the condition (C.KK*) of section 3.2 (and the rule (A.PKK*) of section 2.1) has to be subjected. This qualification was explained informally by saying that the person referred to by *a* must know that he is referred to by it in order for the condition (C.KK*) to be applicable. In a shorter and somewhat elliptical form we might perhaps express the same qualification by saying "*a* knows that he is *a*." It is not quite obvious how this sentence should be formalized. If it were true that the function of the pronoun "he" is simply to stand for its grammatical antecedent, we could translate it by "$K_a(a = a)$." This view of the functions of personal pronouns is misleading, however, as pointed out by Quine,[13] and the translation is worthless: no one can fail to know that the person referred to by *a* (whoever he is or may be) is identical with himself. Rather, we have to say something like "The man who in fact is *a* knows that he is *a*" or, since we have decided to disregard questions of uniqueness, "A man who in fact is *a* knows that he is *a*." The translation of this sentence into our symbolism is "$(Ex)(x = a \ \& \ K_a(x = a))$," which is easily seen to be virtually equivalent to "$(Ex)K_a(x = a)$." This, then, may be expected to serve as the formal counterpart to our qualification, and the condition (C.KK*) may therefore be formulated as follows (disregarding, as we shall henceforth do, the difference between "$(Ex)K_a(x = a)$" and "$(Ex)K_a(a = x)$"):

(C.KK*) If "K_ap" ϵ μ and "$(Ex)K_a(x = a)$" ϵ μ, and if μ^* is an epistemic alternative to μ (with respect to *a*), then "K_ap" ϵ μ^*.

6.13. *"Knowing who" behaves like "knowing that."* There still remain a few rules which epistemic notions seem to follow when they mingle with quantifiers and which we have not yet formulated. Let us first consider the case in which we are dealing with what a certain person—let his name be *a*—knows. (That is, let "K_a" and "P_a" be the only epistemic operators present.) Then the following conditions on model sets and model systems have to be satisfied:

---

[13] *Word and Object*, p. 113.

(C.EK = EK = *) If "$(Ex)K_a(b = x)$" ϵ μ and if μ^* is an epistemic alternative to μ with respect to a, then "$(Ex)K_a(b = x)$" ϵ μ^*.

(C.EK =) If "$(Ex)K_a(b = x)$" ϵ μ, then "$(Ex)(x = b)$" ϵ μ.

The former condition may be defended by arguments similar to those we used to defend (A.PKK*)—in effect (C.KK*)—in the first few sections of Chapter Two. It says, not surprisingly, that "knows who" behaves, as far as the technique of model systems is concerned, exactly in the same way as "knows that." The latter condition is even more obvious. If (C.EK = EK = *) is strongly reminiscent of (C.KK*), so is (C.EK =) of (C.K). Together, the two conditions we just introduced entail a condition which may naturally be called (C.EK = *) and which is obtained from (C.EK = EK = *) by replacing the last clause ' "$(Ex)K_a(b = x)$" ϵ μ^* ' by ' "$(Ex)(x = b)$" ϵ μ^*.' The relation of the resulting condition to (C.EK = EK = *) and to (C.EK =) may be said to be exactly the same as the relation of (C.K*) to (C.KK*) and to (C.K) respectively.[14]

The conditions (C.EK = EK = *) and (C.EK =) may be used to demonstrate that the following sentence is self-sustaining (provided that p contains no epistemic operators different from "K_a" and "P_a"):

(116) "$(Ex)K_a p \supset K_a(Ex)p$."

Intuitively, the self-sustenance of (116) is not surprising. What it says is that if you know *who* does something you *ipso facto* know *that* someone does it.

---

[14] A part of this analogy is that we have to assume the counterpart to (C. =K) for the notion of "knowing who" instead of "knowing that," i.e., we have to adopt the following condition:

(C. =EK =) If "$(Ex)K_a(x = c)$" ϵ μ and if "$a = b$" ϵ μ, then "$(Ex)K_b(x = c)$" ϵ μ.

The demonstration may proceed by our usual reductive strategy:

(117)	"$(Ex)K_a p$" ϵ μ	$\Big\}$	counterassumption, simplified;
(118)	"$P_a(Ux){\sim}p$" ϵ μ		
(119)	"$K_a p(b/x)$" ϵ μ	$\Big\}$	from (117) by (C.E$_{ep}$) or by (108);
(120)	"$(Ex)K_a(b = x)$" ϵ μ		
(121)	"$(Ux){\sim}p$" ϵ μ^*		from (118) by (C.P*);
(122)	"$p(b/x)$" ϵ μ^*		from (119) by (C.K*);
(123)	"$(Ex)K_a(b = x)$" ϵ μ^*		from (120) by (C.EK = EK = *);
(124)	"$(Ex)(x = b)$" ϵ μ^*		from (120) by (C.EK = *);
(125)	"${\sim}p(b/x)$" ϵ μ^*		from (121) and (123) by (C.U$_{ep}$) or from (121) and (124) by (C.U$_o$).

Here (122) and (125) violate (C.$\sim$), thus reducing the counterassumption *ad absurdum*.

The self-sustenance of (116) shows that there is an interesting difference between the logical behavior of the notion of knowledge and that of the notion of necessity toward quantifiers, in spite of the fact that the two are closely similar in many other respects. For the notion of necessity the analogue of (116) is not valid.[15] From the fact alone that there exists an individual which cannot help having a certain property it does not follow that there necessarily is an individual with this property. For the individual first mentioned might conceivably not exist.

In the same way in which the analogues of (C.K*) and of (C.KK*) are valid for '*B*' instead of '*K*' while the analogue of

---

[15] Cf. my paper "Modality and Quantification," *Theoria*, XXVII (1961), 119–128, especially p. 124.

(C.K) is not, in the same way the analogues (C.EB = *) and (C.EB = EB = *) of (C.EK = *) and (C.EK = EK = *) for '*B*' are valid while the analogue of (C.EK =) is not. Since (C.EK =) was not used at all in the argument (117)–(125), the analogue "$(Ex)B_a p \supset B_a(Ex)p$" of (116) for belief instead of knowledge is also self-sustaining, provided of course that *p* does not contain any epistemic operators different from "B_a" and "C_a."

6.14. *Laws of commutation.* The generalizations of (C.EK = EK = *) and of the other conditions which we have just set up to more complicated cases are of technical rather than philosophical interest. I shall therefore forego them here. Instead, it may be instructive to ask whether epistemic operators and quantifiers commute in some way different from that expressed by (116). As far as the operators '*K*' and '*P*' are concerned, the simplest possible types of putative commutation are exemplified by the following sentences (it is assumed that *p* does not contain epistemic operators different from "K_a" and "P_a"):

(126)   "$K_a(Ex)p \supset (Ex)K_a p$,"

(116)   "$(Ex)K_a p \supset K_a(Ex)p$,"

(127)   "$K_a(Ux)p \supset (Ux)K_a p$,"

(128)   "$(Ux)K_a p \supset K_a(Ux)p$."

Of these, (116) was already seen to be self-sustaining. Intuitively, it may be expected that (126) should not turn out to be self-sustaining. If you know that someone has a certain property, it does not always follow that you should know who has it. From the fact that you know that there are spies around it does not follow that you should know who is one. In contrast, (127) may be expected to be self-sustaining. What one knows of *every* man one knows of *each* man.

These expectations turn out to be justified. If we assume that p is an atomic sentence, it does not take long to construct a counterexample to show that (126) is not self-sustaining:

(129) "$K_a(Ex)p$" ϵ μ ⎫
(130) "$(Ux)P_a\sim p$" ϵ μ ⎬ counterassumption, simplified;

(131) "$(Ex)p$" ϵ μ from (129) by (C.K);

(132) "$p(b/x)$" ϵ μ ⎫ from (131) by (C.E$_o$) or
(133) "$(Ex)(x = b)$" ϵ μ ⎬ (C.E$_{ep}$).

There is nothing more we can do here. In order to substitute b for the bound variable of (130) we would need—cf. (109)—an additional premise to the effect that "$(Ex)K_a(b = x)$" ϵ μ. Such a premise is not available, however. In fact, since all our conditions are satisfied, the construction (129)–(133) gives us a counterexample to the self-sustenance of (126).

In contrast, (127) is easily seen to be self-sustaining:

(134) "$K_a(Ux)p$" ϵ μ ⎫ counterassumption, simplified;
(135) "$(Ex)P_a\sim p$" ϵ μ ⎬

(136) "$P_a\sim p(b/x)$" ϵ μ ⎫ from (135) by (C.E$_{ep}$);
(137) "$(Ex)K_a(b = x)$" ϵ μ ⎬

(138) "$\sim p(b/x)$" ϵ μ^* from (136) by (C.P*);

(139) "$(Ex)(x = b)$" ϵ μ^* from (137) by (C.EK = *);

(140) "$(Ux)p$" ϵ μ^* from (134) by (C.K*);

(141) "$p(b/x)$" ϵ μ^* from (139) and (140) by (C.U$_o$).

Here (141) and (138) violate (C.$\sim$). It was assumed in (141) that p contains no epistemic operators. If it contains occurrences of "K_a" or "P_a," we need only to replace (139) by the following step:

(139)$_a$ "$(Ex)K_a(b = x)$" ϵ μ^* from (137) by (C.EK = EK = *);

and to replace, of course, (C.U$_o$) by (C.U$_{ep}$).

Of the different possibilities of commutation, (128) is the most intriguing one. It is quite easy to verify that (128) is not self-sustaining. Hence the distinction between

(142) "$K_a(Ux)p$"

and

(143) "$(Ux)K_ap$"

is important; the former implies the latter, but not vice versa.

Aristotle may have been the first to call attention to a distinction which prima facie may seem exactly the same as ours. In the *Analytica Priora* he says of an expression which may perhaps be rendered in English by "to know of every triangle that it has its angles equal to two right angles" that it is not unambiguous, for it may mean knowledge "either of the universal or of the particulars." [16] The reason why Aristotle's distinction is not the same as ours is apparent from section 6.11: (143) cannot be translated in terms of the phrase "of each man a knows that"; we should rather use some locution like "of each man known to a he knows that." Since it does not imply "$(Ux)p$," we cannot really say it speaks of all men. Hence it can scarcely be relevant to Aristotle's distinction, which rather seems to be that between (142) and

(144) "$(Ux)(Ey)(y = x \ \& \ K_ap(y/x))$"

(cf. section 6.11); (144) is likely to be what is meant by a sen-

---

[16] II, 21, 67^{a}16 ff.; see also *Analytica Posteriora* I, 5, 74^{a}30 ff.

tence of the form "Each man is known by a to be such-and-such," not (143).

The upshot of these remarks is to enhance the reputation of (144) at the expense of that of (143). It therefore becomes as important to inquire into the status of sentences of the form

$$(145) \quad ``K_a(Ux)p \quad \supset \quad (Ux)(Ey)(y = x \ \& \ K_ap(y/x))"$$

and

$$(146) \quad ``(Ux)(Ey)(y = x \ \& \ K_ap(y/x)) \quad \supset \quad K_a(Ux)p"$$

as of those of the form (127) and (128). A sentence of form (145) is not self-sustaining although you may have expected it to be. The reason for this mild counterintuitiveness is intuitive enough: (144) embodies a presupposition which (142) does not, namely, that there is for every man at least one term (say b) referring to him in such a way that it is true to say "a knows who b is." More colloquially, in (144) it is presupposed that everybody is known to the bearer of a while in (142) this assumption is not made. Make an explicit premise of it—say by formulating it as "$(Ux)(Ey)(y = x \ \& \ (Ez)K_a(y = z))$"—and you will find that the self-sustenance of (145) is restored.[17]

What, then, about (146)? If you think of a as a third-person pronoun or as somebody else's name, you will be led to expect that (146) is not self-sustaining. And, as you may verify, this expectation turns out to be right. One may know something about each member of some class without knowing that it holds for all the members; for one may fail to know that one has exhausted the class, that the individuals one knows are all there are in the

---

[17] We are again very close to a point Aristotle makes. In *Analytica Posteriora* I, 1, 71ª31, he gives an example which in effect constitutes a counterinstance to the self-sustenance of (145). His subsequent criticism of a solution "some people offer" suggests that he is not unaware of the distinction between (143) and (144), either.

class.[18] By constructing a counterexample to (146) you may verify that our theory fits to this fact.

But if you think of *a* as the first-person pronoun "I," (146) begins to look much more like a self-sustaining sentence. If I assert that I know something about *each* member of a class, I seem to be asserting *ipso facto* that I know that it holds for *all* the members. A moment's reflection shows why this seems to be so. It may of course happen that I know something about each man without knowing it of all men; somebody else may find out that I do and say so. But even though I may happen to be in such a predicament, I cannot myself know (at the time) that I am in it. Hence asserting (144) in the first person without asserting (142) seems paradoxical—and usually is paradoxical, in a perfectly good sense.

We have already defined this sense. What we have here is one more instance of epistemic implication: although (144) does not virtually imply (142), the former does imply the latter epistemically if *a* is the pronoun "I." This may be demonstrated as follows (we assume for simplicity that there are no epistemic operators in *p*):

---

[18] My point is closely related to Bertrand Russell's remarks on what he calls "limited first-order omniscience" (see *Human Knowledge* [London, 1948], p. 150). One of Russell's examples deals with a wise man who has ascertained of each particular man that he is mortal but who does not know that he has exhausted all men there are and hence does not know that all men are mortal. The state of his knowledge may be described in a way which involves an apparent violation of what we have said in Chapter Five, for it is tempting to say of him that he knows every man to be mortal but does not know that he knows. The violation is only an apparent one, however, for there is a difference between the present case and those studied in Chapter Five. There we argued for a (virtual) implication of the form "$K_a p \supset K_a K_a p$"; here we have to do with counterexamples to an implication which is essentially of the form "$(Ux)K_a p \supset K_a(Ux)K_a p$." The inserted quantifier makes all the difference to the validity (self-sustenance) of the two implications.

(147) "$K_a((Ux)(Ey)(y = x \,\&\, K_a p(y/x))$ counterassump-
         $\&\, P_a(Ex)\sim p)$" ϵ μ tion, simplified;

         "$(Ux)(Ey)(y = x \,\&\, K_a p(y/x))$" ϵ μ⎫ from (147) by
(148) "$P_a(Ex)\sim p$" ϵ μ ⎬ (C.K) and
         ⎭ (C.&);

(149) "$(Ex)\sim p$" ϵ μ^* from (148) by
         (C.P*);

(150) "$((Ux)(Ey)(y = x \,\&\, K_a p(y/x))$" ϵ μ^*⎫ from (147) by
         "$P_a(Ex)\sim p$" ϵ μ^* ⎬ (C.K*) and
         ⎭ (C.&);

(151) "$\sim p(b/x)$" ϵ μ^* ⎫   from (149) by
(152) "$(Ex)(x = b)$" ϵ μ^* ⎬   (C.E$_o$);

(153) "$(Ey)(y = b \,\&\, K_a p(y/x))$" ϵ μ^* from (150) and
         (152) by
         (C.U$_o$);

(154) "$c = b \,\&\, K_a p(c/x)$" ϵ μ^* ⎫   from (153) by
         ⎪ (C.E$_{ep}$) be-
         ⎬ cause here
         "$(Ey)K_a(c = y)$" ϵ μ^* ⎪ $(p(y/x))(c/y)=$
         ⎭ $p(c/x)$;

(155) "$K_a p(c/x)$" ϵ μ^* ⎫   from (154) by
(156) "$(c = b)$" ϵ μ^* ⎬   (C.&);

(157) $p(c/x)$ ϵ μ^* from (155) by
         (C.K);

(158) $p(b/x)$ ϵ μ^* from (156) and
         (157) by the
         extension of
         (C. =).

Here (158) and (151) violate (C.∼), showing what we want to show.

Perhaps it is appropriate that the longest formal argument of this work will remain the last.

A List of Frequently Mentioned Rules, Conditions, and Sentences

Rules:

(A.PKK*)   If a set λ of sentences is defensible and if "$K_a p_1$" ϵ λ, "$K_a p_2$" ϵ λ, . . . , "$K_a p_k$" ϵ λ, "$P_a q$" ϵ λ, then the set {"$K_a p_1$," "$K_a p_2$," . . . , "$K_a p_k$," q} is also defensible.

(A.PK*)   Like (A.PKK*) except that {"$K_a p_1$," "$K_a p_2$," . . . , "$K_a p_k$," q} is replaced by {p_1, p_2, . . . , p_k, q}.

(A.K)   If λ is defensible and if "$K_a p$" ϵ λ, then $\lambda + \{p\}$ is also defensible.

(A.$\sim$K)   If λ is defensible and if "$\sim K_a p$" ϵ λ, then $\lambda + \{$"$P_a \sim p$"$\}$ is also defensible.

(A.$\sim$P)   If λ is defensible and if "$\sim P_a p$" ϵ λ, then $\lambda + \{$"$K_a \sim p$"$\}$ is also defensible.

(A.&)   If λ is defensible and if "p & q" ϵ λ, then $\lambda + \{p, q\}$ is also defensible.

List of Conditions

(A.v)   If λ is defensible and if "p v q" ϵ λ, then $\lambda + \{p\}$ or $\lambda + \{q\}$ is defensible (or both are).

(A.$\sim$)   If p ϵ λ and "$\sim p$" ϵ λ, then λ is indefensible.

(A.$\sim$&)   If "$\sim(p \ \& \ q)$" ϵ λ and if λ is defensible, then so is the set obtained from λ by replacing "$\sim(p \ \& \ q)$" by "$(\sim p$ v $\sim q)$."

(A.$\sim$v)   If "$\sim(p$ v $q)$" ϵ λ and if λ is defensible, then so is the set obtained from λ by replacing "$\sim(p$ v $q)$" by "$(\sim p \ \& \ \sim q)$."

(A.$\sim\sim$)   If "$\sim\sim p$" ϵ λ and if λ is defensible, then so is the set obtained from λ by replacing "$\sim\sim p$" by p.

Conditions:

(C.P*)   If "$P_a p$" ϵ μ and if μ belongs to a model system Ω, then there is in Ω at least one epistemic alternative μ^* to μ (with respect to a) such that p ϵ μ^*.

(C.KK*)   If "$K_a q$" ϵ μ and if μ^* is an epistemic alternative to μ (with respect to a) in some model system, then "$K_a q$" ϵ μ^*.

(C.K*)   If "$K_a p$" ϵ μ and if μ^* is an epistemic alternative to μ (with respect to a) in some model system, then p ϵ μ^*.

(C.K)   If "$K_a p$" ϵ μ, then p ϵ μ.

(C.$\sim$K)   If "$\sim K_a p$" ϵ μ, then "$P_a \sim p$" ϵ μ.

(C.$\sim$P)   If "$\sim P_a p$" ϵ μ, then "$K_a \sim p$" ϵ μ.

List of Conditions

(C.&)   If "p & q" ϵ μ, then p ϵ μ and q ϵ μ.

(C.v)   If "p v q" ϵ μ, then p ϵ μ or q ϵ μ (or both).

(C.~)   If p ϵ μ, then not "$\sim p$" ϵ μ.

(C.~&)   If "$\sim(p$ & $q)$" ϵ μ, then "$\sim p$" ϵ μ or "$\sim q$" ϵ μ (or both).

(C.~v)   If "$\sim(p$ v $q)$" ϵ μ, then "$\sim p$" ϵ μ and "$\sim q$" ϵ μ.

(C.~~)   If "$\sim\sim p$" ϵ μ, then p ϵ μ.

(C.k*)   If "$K_a p$" ϵ μ and if μ belongs to a model system Ω, then there is in Ω at least one epistemic alternative μ^* to μ (with respect to a) such that p ϵ μ^*.

(C.KK*dox)   If "$K_a q$" ϵ μ and if μ^* is a doxastic alternative to μ (with respect to a) in some model system, then "$K_a q$" ϵ μ^*.

(C.BB*ep)   If "$B_a q$" ϵ μ and if μ^* is an epistemic alternative to μ (with respect to a) in some model system, then "$B_a q$" ϵ μ^*.

(C.KB)   If "$K_a q$" ϵ μ, then "$B_a K_a q$" ϵ μ.

(C.dox)   Every doxastic alternative is also an epistemic alternative (with respect to the same free individual symbol).

(C.BK)   If "$B_a q$" ϵ μ, then "$K_a B_a q$" ϵ μ.

(C.E)   If "$(Ex)p$" ϵ μ, then $p(a/x)$ ϵ μ for at least one free individual symbol a.

(C.U)   If "$(Ux)p$" ϵ μ and if b occurs in at least one member of μ, then $p(b/x)$ ϵ μ.

List of Conditions

(C.~E) If "$\sim(Ex)p$" ϵ μ, then "$(Ux)\sim p$" ϵ μ.

(C.~U) If "$\sim(Ux)p$" ϵ μ, then "$(Ex)\sim p$" ϵ μ.

(C.E₀) If "$(Ex)p$" ϵ μ, then $p(a/x)$ ϵ μ and "$(Ex)(x = a)$" ϵ μ for at least one free individual symbol a.

(C.U₀) If "$(Ux)p$" ϵ μ and if "$(Ey)(b=y)$" ϵ μ or "$(Ey)(y = b)$" ϵ μ, then $p(b/x)$ ϵ μ.

(C. =) If p ϵ μ, "$a = b$" ϵ μ, if p is an atomic formula or an identity, and if q is like p except that a and b have been interchanged in one or several places, then q ϵ μ.

(C. = !) Like (C. =) except that it is not limited to atomic formulas and identities.

(C.self≠) For no free individual symbol a, "$a \neq a$" ϵ μ.

(C.self=) If a occurs in the formulas of μ, "$a = a$" ϵ μ.

(C. = K) If "$K_a p$" ϵ μ and "$a = b$" ϵ μ, then "$K_b p$" ϵ μ.

(C. = P) If "$P_a p$" ϵ μ and "$a = b$" ϵ μ, then "$P_b p$" ϵ μ.

(108) If "$(Ex)p$" ϵ μ, then for at least one free individual symbol a we have $p(a/x)$ ϵ μ and "$(Ex)K_b(a = x)$" ϵ μ, provided that there are in p no epistemic operators different from "K_b" and "P_b" and that x occurs within the scope of one of them in p.

(109)   If "$(Ux)p$" ϵ μ and "$(Ey)K_b(a = y)$" ϵ μ, then $p(a/x)$ ϵ μ, provided that there are in p no epistemic operators different from "K_b" and "P_b."

(C.E$_{ep}$)   Like (108) except that the role of "$(Ex)K_b(a = x)$" is played by all the auxiliary formulas of p with respect to x and that the "provided"-clause now runs as follows: provided that there are no bound variables as subscripts of epistemic operators in p.

(C.U$_{ep}$)   Like (109) except that the role of "$(Ey)K_b(a = y)$" is played by a set of formulas which includes each auxiliary formula of p (with respect to x) or at least one of its variants and that the "provided"-clause is modified in the same way as in (C.E$_{ep}$).

(C.EK = EK = *)   If "$(Ex)K_a(b = x)$" ϵ μ and if μ^* is an epistemic alternative to μ with respect to a, then "$(Ex)K_a(b = x)$" ϵ μ^*.

(C.EK = *)   Like (C.EK = EK = *) except that "$(Ex)K_a(b = x)$" ϵ μ^* is replaced by "$(Ex)(x = b)$" ϵ μ^*.

(C.EK =)   If "$(Ex)K_a(b = x)$" ϵ μ, then "$(Ex)(x = b)$" ϵ μ.

(C. = EK =)   If "$(Ex)K_a(x = c)$" ϵ μ and if "$a = b$" ϵ μ, then "$(Ex)K_b(x = c)$" ϵ μ.

(C.KK *)(qualified form)   If "$K_a p$" ϵ μ and "$(Ex)K_a(x = a)$" ϵ μ, and if μ^* is an epistemic alternative to μ (with respect to a), then "$K_a p$" ϵ μ^*.

List of Sentences

In the last five conditions the order of identities—for instance, '$(b=x)$' as compared with '$(x=b)$'—may, and must, be disregarded.

Sentences:

(1)   "a knows that p."

(2)   "a knows whether p."

(3)   "a does not know that p."

(4)   "a does not know whether p."

(5)   "a believes that p."

(6)   "It is possible, for all that a knows, that p."

(7)   "It is compatible with everything a believes that p."

(2*)   "$K_a p$ v $K_a \sim p$."

(3*)   "p & $\sim K_a p$."

(4*)   "$\sim K_a p$ & $\sim K_a \sim p$."

(8)   "p but I do not believe that p."

(9)   "p but I do not know whether p."

(8)(a)   "p but a does not believe that p."

(30)   "I believe that the case is as follows: p but I do not believe that p."

(30)*   "$B_a(p$ & $\sim B_a p)$."

(30)(a) "I believe that the case is as follows: p but a does not believe that p."

(30)(a)* "$B_b(p$ & $\sim B_a p)$."

(40)   "I know that the case is as follows: p but I do not know whether p."

(40)*   "$K_a(p$ & $\sim K_a p$ & $\sim K_a \sim p)$."

(41)   "$K_a(p$ & $\sim K_a p)$."

(60)   "I know that I know that p."

(62)   "I know that p."

(63)   "$K_a K_a p$."

(64)   "$K_a p$."

(70)   "a knows that p but he does not know that he knows."

Index of Authors

Index of Authors

Moore, G. E., 9, 64, 78, 95–96

Ohmann, Richard M., 116
Onions, C. T., 13

Parmenides, 22
Peirce, C. S., 93
Plato, 22, 39, 93, 107
Porter, Lord, 38
Prichard, H. A., 108–110, 114–115, 121–122

Quine, W. V. O., 4, 130, 138, 142–144, 150–154, 156–159

Russell, Bertrand, 64, 166

Ryle, Gilbert, 57, 95, 111–112

Schilpp, P. A. (ed.), 64
Schopenhauer, Arthur, 108–110
Sellars, W. (ed.), 110
Socrates, 106
Spinoza, Baruch de, 108, 114–115, 121–122

Taylor, Richard, 108
Tennessen, Herman, 64

Urmson, J. O., 19, 21, 116

Wilson, John Cook, 108
Wittgenstein, Ludwig, 64, 94, 98

Index of Subjects